EURIPIDES · III

Hecuba
Andromache
The Trojan Women
Ion

THE COMPLETE GREEK TRAGEDIES

Edited by David Grene and Richmond Lattimore

EURIPIDES · III

HECUBA
Translated by William Arrowsmith

ANDROMACHE
Translated by John Frederick Nims

THE TROJAN WOMEN
Translated by Richmond Lattimore

ION
Translated by Ronald Frederick Willetts

THE UNIVERSITY OF CHICAGO PRESS

CHICAGO & LONDON

THE UNIVERSITY OF CHICAGO PRESS, CHICAGO 60637

The University of Chicago Press, Ltd., London

ISBN: 0-226-30782-4
LCN: 55-5787

14 13 12 11 10 09 08   23 24 25 26

♾ The paper used in this publication meets the minimum re-
quirements of the American National Standard for Information
Sciences—Permanence of Paper for Printed Library Materials,
ANSI Z39.48-1992.

TABLE OF CONTENTS

HECUBA

Translated by William Arrowsmith

INTRODUCTION TO *HECUBA*

A LONG with Croesus, Oedipus, and Priam, the figure of Hecuba, the *mater dolorosa* of Troy transformed by suffering into the "bitch of Cynossema," survives in classical imagination as a supreme example of the severest degradation the reversal of human fortune can inflict. From Euripides on, through Ovid, medieval literature, and Dante to the "mobled queen" of Hamlet's players, the image persists with extraordinary purity, untampered with, almost unchanged. What Euripides may have taken from his own presumptive source, the lost epic on the sack of Troy by the eighth-century Arctinus of Miletus, we have no way of knowing; but between Euripides and Ovid,[1] very little has been lost, and between Euripides and Dante so little has been lost that the essential experience of the Greek *Hecuba* is still vivid in two compressed tercets of the *Inferno:*[2]

> Ecuba, trista, misera e cattiva,
> poscia che vide Polissena morta,
> e del suo Polidoro in su la riva
>
> del mar si fu la dolorosa accorta,
> forsennata latrò sì come cane:
> tanto il dolor le fe' la mente torta.

Whether this persistence of the image derives from the myth or the play hardly matters; but the purity with which it persists argues, I suppose, as much the power of the original play as the authority of Ovid who transcribed it for later literature. Ovid is normally nothing if not fickle with his sources, but in this case he was working with a celebrated play and a myth so standardized in its Euripidean version as to prove intractable. But either through Greek or, via Ovid, through Latin, the Euripidean Hecuba has left to subsequent literatures an authoritative and compelling image of human suffering under the reversal of fortune.

1. *Metamorphoses* xiii. 407 ff.
2. Canto xxx, ll. 16–21: "Hecuba, sad, miserable and captive, after she had seen Polyxena slain, and, forlorn, discerned her Polydorus on the shore of the sea, barked like a dog, out of her senses: to such a degree had the sorrow wrung her soul."

To a large degree this authority was quickened by the high esteem and even popularity which the *Hecuba* enjoyed for more than two thousand years. Admired, much quoted and echoed in antiquity, it became one of the favorite plays of the Byzantine schoolbooks, was translated by Erasmus into Latin, and was finally almost canonized as a model of tragedy by the French classical dramatists. But in the nineteenth century the *Hecuba*, in a peripety as sudden and undeserved as that of its protagonist, fell into a profound disfavor, which has never been withdrawn; indeed, it is still commonly cited by handbooks, those tidy morgues of leached opinion, as one of the feeblest, if not the feeblest, of surviving Greek plays. The cause of this demotion—one which overtook the bulk of Euripides' plays as well—was twofold: first, the persistent misconception, based on too humble or too literal a reading of Aristotle, that Sophoclean structure provides the ideal norm of Greek tragic structure; second, a killing misunderstanding of the political experience of the play and what the logic of political necessity does to the characters. The consequence of the first has been to snarl Euripides' meaning by hopelessly disfiguring his form, while the second has operated to cut off our access to a range and power of experience which Euripides, alone of the Greek tragedians, shares with the twentieth century.

But the *Hecuba*, if it is not a great play, is at least a moving and a powerful one, a taut, bitter little tragedy of the interrelationships between those who hold power and those who suffer it. And, far from lacking unity or formal coherence—though its unity is anything but Aristotelian—it is in fact a tightly constructed tragedy, driving home with great economy and control its central tragic idea. Superficially, the action is episodic; like the *Heracles*, it consists of two separate actions joined together without causal connection. Over both actions—the slaughter of Polyxena by the Greeks and the discovery of the body of Polydorus which leads to Hecuba's atrocious revenge on Polymestor—the figure of the suffering Hecuba loosely presides, giving at least the feel of unity to the various episodes as they occur. Carefully, if not elaborately, her progress, from grief to despair, toward the final atrocity is traced under the rhythm of the descending blows, each one heavier than the last; but the emphasis is not so much on the psychology of the change within Hecuba as the way in which, confronted by her tormentors, she is forced to yield, one by one, her values, her self-respect, and the faith which makes her human. If what she suffers dehumanizes her, Euripides' emphasis is centered at least as much on *what* she suffers, its rationale, its cost, its significance, as on the anguish of the suffering itself. And, for this reason, though Hecuba provides a convenient focus for the play, whose episodes and values converge around her, her figure does not suffice to give the play unity or to make of it a tragedy of character.

Like so many Euripidean plays, the *Hecuba* is not the tragedy of an individual but a group tragedy, its apparently random and disconnected episodes bound together by a single overriding idea, forced up in ever more inclusive complexity by the development of the action. Uniting the *Hecuba*, underlying Hecuba's transformation, and joining persecutors and persecuted alike in a common tragedy is a bleak logic of political necessity, a concern that brings the *Hecuba* close to the *Trojan Women* and Thucydides' Melian Dialogue. Those characters who urge that necessity leaves them no choice are as corrupted by their own logic as those who, like Hecuba and the Chorus, suffer it. Confronted by the fact of power which makes her helpless, Hecuba, like the Melians, can only plead honor, decency, the gods, the moral law (*nomos*); when these appeals fail, what is civilized in her fails with them, and she takes a revenge so hideously brutal that we know, even before Polymestor, himself brutalized by suffering, predicts her transformation into the "bitch of Cynossema," that her humanity has been destroyed. Blow by blow, her hold on her humanity weakens: it is this loss of purchase that explains her sophistic approval of pure persuasion and her appeal to Agamemnon to repay his nights with Cassandra. In the end, she passes beyond the reach of judgment, for no moral judgment is pertinent when the denial of justice has destroyed her human and moral skills alike. At the same time, Hecuba's tormentors are corrupted by their commitment to their own logic: Odysseus involved in private dishonor for public reasons; Agamemnon emptying the meaning of human justice by enforcing justice only when his reputation is threatened.

But there is more to it than that. Necessity—what it is, when it arises, what it entails in action—is not easy to know, especially from the point of view of those who hold power. But just because necessity is hard and because the justification it gives—in politics, in love, in war—is unanswerable, it is the justification most frequently debased. And in the *Hecuba*, which is a tragedy and not a melodrama, it is this difficult and tragic aspect of necessity which interests Euripides. Hecuba is not tormented by the calculating cruelty of two vicious politicians but is a victim of men in the process of corruption by a power whose real necessities they understand no better than their own real motives. For what they do they claim the justification that they cannot act otherwise. In actuality, they do not act from necessity, but the excuse of necessity cloaks their fear. And just as Thucydides, by setting his Melian Dialogue on the strategically unimportant island of Melos, undercuts the Athenian generals' justification of necessity, so Euripides, by introducing Talthybius to pity Hecuba and to describe the soldiers' admiration for Polyxena's courage, undercuts the whole force of Odysseus' and Agamemnon's arguments, all based on the mistaken premise of the insensitivity of the mass to moral considerations. In the disparity between the facts and their arguments justice withers, while the callous shifting of responsibility from those in power to the mass dooms political life by depriving it of either trust or the illusion of moral action.

Within this binding framework of necessity, the characters are presented with severe economy. Hecuba herself is not so much character as an image of character in the process of annihilation. Odysseus is a demagogue by conviction (and hence all the more dangerous), decisive in action, alive to compassion but not to the point of allowing it to affect considerations which, because they are political, he thinks are beyond the reach of morality. Agamemnon, less arrogant than Odysseus, is weak, vacillating for the same reason that Odysseus is decisive, and enormously sensitive to the figure he cuts. But both alike, confident in their crude estimate of their necessities and driven by the same fear, compound the tragedy, forfeiting to their own power their freedom of moral action and as enslaved by their misguided notion of their necessities as Hecuba by her real necessity. Polymestor, alone of the characters in the play, has no necessity; he acts from crude greed and is a stark picture of barbarian viciousness. Opposite him, as virtuous as he is corrupt, stands Polyxena, almost too noble to be true. But Euripides' point is surely that it is only extreme youth and extreme innocence which can afford the illusion of total commitment. Like so many of Euripides' self-sacrificing young heroes, her death, futile in itself, exposes, by the quality of its commitment, the dense ambiguity of the moral atmosphere for those who cannot die.

What, finally, of justice and the gods? To this question the *Hecuba* makes no answer; if the action proves anything, it proves precisely the impossibility of making an answer. In the collision of their powers and necessities and purposes, men and women suffer; their appeals to *nomos* and the gods may be answered or not. Thus, at the close of the play, Polymestor predicts Agamemnon's death in Argos, and so hints at justice from heaven. But it is the very lag between crime and heaven's punishment of it, the apparent carelessness of the gods in the face of human anguish, that indicts any firm answer. Stubbornly, bleakly, rightly, the play refuses to annul the honesty of its experience on behalf of the time-honored theodicy, hinting merely that if there are powers beyond man, their justice is so alien, so slow, so indifferent, as to make impossible even the hope of communication or understanding. But man continues to demand justice and an order with which he can live, and it is the nobility of this demand, maintained against the whole tenor of his experience, in the teeth of the universal indifference and the inconsistency of fortune, that in Euripides makes man tragic. His suffering is limited only by his hope; take away his hope, as Hecuba's was taken, and he forfeits his humanity, destroyed by the hideous gap between his illusion and the intolerable reality.

The Date

The date of the *Hecuba* is uncertain, but the play may be reasonably assigned to the year 425–424. At least line 173 of the play is parodied by Aristophanes in the *Clouds* (423 B.C.) and line 462 refers to the establishment of the Delian Games by the Athenians in

426. The background of the Archidamian War helps to explain the choral emphasis on the tragic waste of war, as well as the concern of the play with the logic of imperial necessity. It is my personal conviction that the *Hecuba* was one of three tragedies for which the extant *Cyclops* was performed as the satyr-play. The connections in theme, treatment, and character are extremely close, especially in the blinding of Polymestor and Polyphemus.

CHARACTERS

Ghost of Polydorus

Hecuba

Chorus of captive Trojan women

Polyxena

Odysseus

Talthybius

Maidservant of Hecuba

Agamemnon

Polymestor, king of Thracian Chersonese

Sons of Polymestor

For Marshall Van Deusen

HECUBA

SCENE: *The shore of the Thracian Chersonese. Pavilioned tents, the quarters of the Trojan women, stand in the background. The time is just before dawn. Enter above,* ex machina, *the ghost of Polydorus.*

Polydorus
Back from the pit of the dead, from the somber door
that opens into hell, where no god goes,
I have come,
        the ghost of Polydorus,
son and last surviving heir of Hecuba
and Priam, king of Troy.
              My father, fearing
that Troy might fall to the assembled arms of Hellas,   5
had me conveyed in secret out of danger
sending me here to Thrace, to Polymestor,
who rules this fertile plain of Chersonese
and curbs with harsh power a nation of horsemen.
With me my father sent a sum of gold,   10
intending that, if Troy should someday fall,
his living sons might be provided for.
Being the youngest, I was chosen, still too small
and slight to carry arms or throw a spear.   15
But as long as Troy's great ramparts stood proud
and unbreached, so long as our towers held intact
and Hector, my brother, prospered in the fighting,
I flourished under the care of my father's friend,
a green shoot thriving under his watchful eye.   20
But when Troy fell and Hector died,
and picks and shovels rooted up our hearth,
and there, by the altar that Apollo's hands once built,
Priam fell, butchered by Achilles' son,
then my father's friend took off his mask,

and moved by nothing more than simple greed, 25
murdered me and threw my body to the sea.
Here, pounded by the surf, my corpse still lies,
carried up and down on the heaving swell of the sea,
unburied and unmourned.
                          Disembodied now,
I hover as a wraith over my mother's head, 30
riding for three long days upon the air,
three hopeless days of suffering and fear
since she left Troy and came to Chersonese.
Here on the shore of Thrace, in sullen idleness
beside its ships, the whole Achaean army waits 35
and cannot sail. For Achilles' ghost appeared,
stalking on his tomb, wailing, and stopped the ships
as they stood out for sea on the journey home.
He demanded my sister Polyxena as prize, 40
the blood of the living to sweeten a dead man's grave.
And he shall have her, a prize of honor and a gift
bestowed upon him by his friends. On this day
destiny shall take my sister down to death.
And you, poor Mother, you must see 45
your two last children dead this day,
my sister slaughtered and my unburied body
washed up on shore at the feet of a slave.
These were the favors I asked of the gods below—
to find my mother and be buried by her hands— 50
and they have granted my request.
                          Now I go,
for there below I see my mother coming,
stumbling from Agamemnon's tent, still shaken
by that dream in which she saw my ghost.

(Enter Hecuba from the tent. At the entrance she crumples to the
ground, and stretches out her hands to the three or four
Trojan women who stand beside her in the tent.)

—O Mother,   55
poor majesty, old fallen queen,
shorn of greatness, pride, and everything but life,
which leaves you slavery and bitterness
and lonely age.
                    Some god destroys you now,
exacting in your suffering the cost
for having once been happy in this life.

Hecuba

O helplessness of age!
Too old, too weak, to stand—
Help me, women of Troy.   60
Give this slave those hands
you offered to her once
when she was queen of Troy.
Prop me with your arms   65
and help these useless
stumbling legs to walk.

O star of morning,
    light of Zeus
    shining in the night!
    What apparition rose,
what shape of terror stalking the darkness?   70

O goddess Earth,
    womb of dreams
    whose dusky wings
trouble, like bats, the flickering air!

Beat back that dream I dreamed,
that horror that rose in the night, those phantoms of children,
my son Polydorus in Thrace, Polyxena, my daughter!   75
    Call back that vision of horror!

O gods who protect this land,
    preserve my son, save him,
    the last surviving anchor of my house,   80

still holding in the snows of Thrace,
still warded by his father's friend!

Disaster I dreamed,
terror on terror!
Never has my heart   85
so shivered with fear!

O Helenus, I need you now,
interpreter of dreams!
Help me, Cassandra,
help me read my dreams!
I saw a little doe, a dappled doe, torn from between my knees,   90
cruelly ripped away, mangled by a wolf with blood-red nails!

And then fresh terror rose:
I saw Achilles' ghost
stalk upon his tomb, howling,
demanding a prize
from the wretched women of Troy.   95

O gods, I implore you,
beat back this dream,
preserve my children!

(*Enter chorus of captive Trojan women.*
They speak individually.)

Chorus
—We come to you in haste,
  Hecuba.

—   We left the tents . . .

—where the lot assigned us.   100

—Slaves, torn from home
  when Troy was burnt and sacked
  by the conquering Greeks!

—We bring you painful news.   105

—We cannot lighten your load.

—We bring you worse to bear.

—Just now, in full assembly,
  the Greek decree came down.

—They voted your daughter must die . . .

—to be slaughtered alive

—on the tomb of Achilles!

—The sails had been unfurled,
  and the fleet stood out to sea,
  when from his tomb Achilles rose,   110
  armor blazing, and held them back,
  crying:
 "Ho, Argives, where do you sail,
  leaving my grave unhonored?"   115

—Waves of argument broke loose,
  dividing Greek from Greek.
  If one man spoke for death,
  another spoke against it.

—On your behalf spoke Agamemnon,   120
  lover of your daughter,
  poor, mad Cassandra.

—Then the two sons of Theseus,
  twin shoots of Athens, rose and spoke,
  but both with one intent—   125
  to crown Achilles' grave
  with living blood, asking
  if Cassandra's love meant more
  than the courage of Achilles.

—And so the struggle swayed,   130
  equally poised—

—   Until *he* spoke—
  that hypocrite with honeyed tongue,
  that demagogue Odysseus.
  And in the end he won,
  asking what one slave was worth   135

when laid in the balance
with the honor of Achilles.

—He wouldn't have the dead
descending down to Hades
telling tales of Greek
ingratitude to Greeks
who fell for Hellas
on the foreign field of Troy.   140

—And he is coming here
to tear your daughter from your breast
and wrench her from your arms.

—Go to the temples!

—   Go to the shrines

—Fall at Agamemnon's knees!   145

—Call on heaven's gods!

—Invoke the gods below!

—Unless your prayers prevent her death,
unless your pleas can keep her safe,
then you shall see your child,   150
face downward on the earth
and the stain in the black earth spread
    as the red blood drops
from the gleaming golden chain
that lies broken at her throat.

Hecuba
O grief!
        What can I say?
What are the words for loss?   155

O bitterness of age,
slavery not to be borne,
unendurable pain!
To whom can I turn?   160
Childless and homeless,

my husband murdered,
my city stained with fire. . . .
Where can I go?
What god in heaven,
what power below
will help me now?
O women of Troy,   165
heralds of evil,
bringers of loss,
this news you bring is my sentence of death.
Why should I live? How live in the light
when its goodness is gone,
when all I have is grief?
Bear me up,
poor stumbling feet,   170
and take me to the tent.

> (*She stumbles painfully to Agamemnon's tent and then
> cries out in terror to Polyxena within.*)

O my child!
        Polyxena,
step from the tent!
Come and hear the news
your wretched mother brings,
this news of horror   175
that touches your life!

> (*Enter from the tent Polyxena, a beautiful young girl.*)

Polyxena
   That terror in your voice!
   That cry of fear
   flushing me forth
   like a bird in terror!

Hecuba
   O my child! My baby. . . .   180

Polyxena
   Again that cry! Why?

Hecuba
    I am afraid for you—

Polyxena
    Tell me the truth, Mother.
    No, I am afraid. Something
    in your face frightens me.   185

Hecuba
    O my child! My child—

Polyxena
    You *must* tell me, Mother.

Hecuba
    A dreadful rumor came.
    Some Greek decree   190
    that touches your life—

Polyxena
    Touches my life how?
    For god's sake, Mother,
    speak!

Hecuba
        —The Greeks,
    in full assembly,
    have decreed your death,
    a living sacrifice   195
    upon Achilles' tomb.

Polyxena
    O my poor mother!
    How I pity you,
    this broken-hearted life
    of pain!
        What god
    could make you suffer so,
    impose such pain,   200
    such grief in one poor life?
    Alive, at least

I might have shared
your slavery with you,
my unhappy youth
with your embittered age.
But now I die,
and you must see my death:—
butchered like a lamb   205
squalling with fright,
and the throat held taut
for the gashing knife,
and the gaping hole
where the breath of life
goes out,
   and sinks
downward into dark
with the unconsolable dead.   210

It is *you* I pity,
Mother.
   For *you* I cry.
Not for myself,
     not for this life
whose suffering is such
I do not care to live,
but call it happiness to die.   215

Coryphaeus
 Look, Hecuba. Odysseus is coming here
 himself. There must be news.

     (*Enter Odysseus, attended by several soldiers.*)

Odysseus
      By now, Hecuba,
 I think you know what decision the army has taken
 and how we voted.
     But let me review the facts.
 By majority vote the Greeks have decreed as follows: 220
 your daughter, Polyxena, must die as a victim

and prize of honor for the grave of Achilles.
The army has delegated me to act as escort.
Achilles' son will supervise the rite
and officiate as priest.

There matters rest.
You understand your position? You must not attempt   225
to hold your daughter here by force, nor,
I might add, presume to match your strength with mine.
Remember your weakness and accept this tragic loss
as best you can.

Nothing you do or say
can change the facts. Under the circumstances,
the logical course is resignation.

Hecuba

O gods,
is there no end to this ordeal of suffering,   230
this struggle with despair?

Why do I live?
I should have died, died long ago.
But Zeus preserved me, saved me, kept me alive
to suffer, each time to suffer worse
than all the grief that went before.

Odysseus,
if a slave may put her question to the free—
without intent to hurt or give offense—   235
then let me ask you one brief question now
and hear your answer.

Odysseus

Ask me your question.
I can spare you the time.

Hecuba

Do you remember once
how you came to Troy, a spy, in beggar's disguise,   240
smeared with filth, in rags, and tears of blood
were streaming down your beard?

Odysseus

                             I remember
the incident. It left its mark on me.

Hecuba

But Helen penetrated your disguise
and told me who you were? Told *me* alone?

Odysseus

I stood, I remember, in danger of death.

Hecuba

And how humble you were? How you fell at my knees   245
and begged for life?

Odysseus

                And my hand almost froze on your dress.

Hecuba

And you were at my mercy, *my* slave then.
Do you remember what you said?

Odysseus

                     Said?
Anything I could. Anything to live.

Hecuba

And I let you have your life? I set you free?

Odysseus

Because of what you did, I live today.   250

Hecuba

Then can you say your treatment now of me
is not contemptible? To take from me
what you confess you took, and in return
do everything you can to do me wrong
and ruin me?
              O gods, spare me the sight   255
of this thankless breed, these politicians
who cringe for favors from a screaming mob

and do not care what harm they do their friends,
providing they can please a crowd!

                        Tell me,
on what feeble grounds can you justify   260
your vote of death?

                 Political necessity?
But how? And do your politics require
the shedding of human blood upon a grave,
where custom calls for cattle?

                     Or is it vengeance
that Achilles' ghost demands, death for his death,
and exacts of her? But what has she to do
with his revenge? Who ever hurt him less
than this poor girl? If death is what he wants,   265
let Helen die. He went to Troy for *her;*
for *her* he died.

             Or is it merely looks
that you require, some surpassing beauty in a girl
whose dying loveliness might appease the hurt
of this fastidious ghost? Then do not look
for loveliness from us. Look to Helen,
loveliest of lovely women on this earth
by far—lovely Helen, who did him harm   270
far more than we.

             So much by way of answer
to the justice of your case.

               Now, Odysseus,
I present my claim for your consideration,
my just demand for payment of your debt
of life.

        You admit yourself you took my hand;
you knelt at my feet and begged for life.

                      But see—

     (Hecuba kneels at the feet of Odysseus and takes his hand.)
now I touch you back as you touched me.   275

I kneel before you on the ground and beg
for mercy back:
                    Let her stay with me.
Let her live.
                    Surely there are dead enough
without her death. And everything I lost
lives on in her. This one life   280
redeems the rest. She is my comfort, my Troy,
my staff, my nurse; she guides me on my way.
She is all I have.
                    And you have power,
Odysseus, greatness and power. But clutch them gently,
use them kindly, for power gives no purchase
to the hand, it will not hold, soon perishes,
and greatness goes.
                    I know. I too was great
but I am nothing now. One day   285
cut down my greatness and my pride.
                                    But I implore you,
Odysseus, be merciful, take pity on me!
Go to the Greeks. Argue, coax them, convince them
that what they do is wrong. Accuse them of murder!
Tell them we are helpless, we are women,
the same women whom they tore from sanctuary   290
at the altars. But they pitied us, they spared us then.
Plead with them.
                    Read them your law of murder. Tell them how
it applies to slave and free without distinction.
But go.
            Even if your arguments were weak,
if you faltered or forgot your words, it would not matter.
Of themselves that power, that prestige you have
would guarantee success, swelling in your words,
and borrowing from what you are a resonance and force   295
denied to less important men.

Coryphaeus
                          Surely
no man could be so callous or so hard of heart
he could hear this mother's heartbroken cry
and not be touched.

Odysseus
                    Allow me to observe, Hecuba,
that in your hysterics you twist the facts.

                                    First,
I am not, as you fondly suppose, your enemy,   300
and my advice, believe me, was sincerely and kindly meant.
I readily admit, moreover, the extent of my debt—
everything I am today I owe to you.
And in return I stand ready and willing
to honor my debt by saving your life. Indeed,
I have never suggested otherwise.

                              But note:
I said *your* life, not your daughter's life,
a very different matter altogether.
I gave my word that when we captured Troy   305
your daughter should be given to our best soldier
as a prize upon request. That was my promise,
a solemn public commitment which I intend to keep.
Besides, there is a principle at stake
and one, moreover, in whose neglect or breach
governments have fallen and cities come to grief,
because their bravest, their most exceptional men,
received no greater honor than the common run.
And Achilles deserves our honor far more than most,
a great man and a great soldier who died greatly   310
for his country.
                Tell me, what conduct could be worse
than to give your friend a lifetime of honor and respect
but neglect him when he dies?
                            And what then,
if war should come again and we enlist our citizens

to serve? Would we fight or would we look to our lives,   315
seeing that dead men get no honor?
                              No:
for my lifetime give me nothing more than what I need;
I ask no more. But as regards my grave,
I hope for honor, since honor in the grave
has eternity to run.   320
                    You speak of pity,
but I can talk of pity too. Pity *us*,
pity our old people, those old men and women
no less miserable than yours, the wives and mothers
of all those brave young men who found a grave
in the dust of Troy.
                         Endure; bear your losses,   325
and if you think me wrong to honor courage
in a man, then call me callous.
                          But what of you,
you foreigners who refuse your dead their rights
and break your faith with friends? And then you wonder
that Hellas should prosper while your countries suffer   330
the fates they deserve!

Coryphaeus
                     This is what it means
to be a slave: to be abused and bear it,
compelled by violence to suffer wrong.

Hecuba
                              O my child,
all my prayers are lost, thrown away   335
on the empty air!
                    So try your powers now.
Implore him, use every skill that pity has,
every voice. Be like the nightingale,
touch him, move him! Fall at his knees,
beg him for life!
                    Even he has children too   340
and may pity them in you.

Polyxena

                  I see your hand,
Odysseus, hidden in the folds of your robes and your face
averted, lest I try to touch your hand or beard
and beg for life.

                Have no fear. You are safe
from me.

            I shall not call on Zeus who helps   345
the helpless.

             I shall not beg for life.

                     No:
I go with you because I must, but most
because I wish to die. If I refuse,
I prove myself a coward, in love with life.   350
But why should I live?

             I had a father once,
king of Phrygia. And so I started life,
a princess of the blood, nourished on lovely hopes
to be a bride for kings. And suitors came
competing for the honor of my hand, while over the girls
and women of Troy, I stood acknowledged mistress,
courted and envied by all, all but a goddess,   355
though bound by death.

             And now I am a slave.
It is that name of slave, so ugly, so strange,
that makes me want to die. Or should I live
to be knocked down to a bidder, sold to a master   360
for cash? Sister of Hector, sister of princes,
doing the work of a drudge, kneading the bread
and scrubbing the floors, compelled to drag out
endless weary days? And the bride of kings,
forced by some low slave from god knows where   365
to share his filthy bed?

              Never.
With eyes still free, I now renounce the light
and dedicate myself to death.

Odysseus,
lead me off. For I see nothing in this life
to give me hope, and nothing here at all   370
worth living for.
                          As for you, Mother,
do nothing, say nothing now to hinder me.
Help me instead; help me to die, now,
before I live disgraced.
                          I am a novice   375
to this life of shame, whose yoke I might endure,
but with such pain that I prefer to die
than go on living.

Coryphaeus
                          Nobility of birth
is a stamp and seal, conspicuous and sharp.   380
But true nobility allied to birth
is a greatness and a glory.

Hecuba
                          I am proud of you,
my child, so very proud, but anguish sticks
in this nobility.
                          If your Achilles
must have his victim, Odysseus, if you
have any care for your own honor left,   385
then let her live. Let me take her place
upon the tomb; kill *me*, be merciless
to *me*, not her. For I gave birth to Paris
whose arrows brought Achilles down.

Odysseus
                                        The ghost
demanded this girl's blood, not yours,   390
old woman.

Hecuba
                Then let me die with her at least,
and we shall be a double drink of blood
for earth and this demanding ghost below.

Odysseus
Her death will do. One victim is required,   395
no more.

Hecuba
                    I *must* die with her! I *must*!

Odysseus
Must? A strong word, Hecuba. It was my impression
I was the master here.

Hecuba
                              I shall stick to her
like ivy to the oak.

Odysseus
                    Take my advice, Hecuba.
For your own good, do not.

Hecuba
                                        Never, never   400
will I let her go.

Odysseus
                    While I, for my part,
refuse to leave her here.

Polyxena
                              Mother, listen.
And you, Odysseus, be gentle with a mother's love.
She has reasons for despair.
                              Poor Mother,
do not struggle with those stronger than you.
Is this what you want—to be thrown down in the dust,   405
this poor old body bruised, shouldered away,
hustled off by younger and stronger arms?
They will do it. No, this is not for you.
O Mother, Mother,
                    give me your hand,
and put your cheek to mine for one last kiss   410
and then no more. For the last, last time

I look upon this gleaming circle of the sun
and speak the last words I shall ever say.
O Mother, Mother,
           now I go below—

Hecuba

Leaving me to live, a slave in the light—   415

Polyxena

Unmarried to my death, no wedding-songs for me—

Hecuba

The song of mourning for you, wretchedness for me—

Polyxena

To lie in the dark with Hades, far from you—

Hecuba

O gods, where can I go? Where shall I die?

Polyxena

I was born to freedom and I die a slave.   420

Hecuba

Fifty children I once had, and all are dead.

Polyxena

What message shall I take to Priam and Hector?

Hecuba

Tell them this: I am the queen of sorrow.

Polyxena

O sweet breasts that nourished me!

Hecuba

So wrong, so wrong! So young to die!   425

Polyxena

Farewell, Cassandra! Mother, farewell—

Hecuba

Let others fare well. I never shall.

Polyxena

Goodbye, Polydorus, my brother in Thrace—

Hecuba
> If he lives at all—for all I have is loss.

Polyxena
> He lives. He shall close your dying eyes.   430

Hecuba
> I died of sorrow while I was still alive.

Polyxena
> Shroud my head, Odysseus, and lead me out.
> Even before I die, my cries have broken
> my mother's heart, and she has broken mine.
> O light of day!
>   I still can cry the light   435
> in that little space of life I have to live
> before I die upon Achilles' tomb!

> > (*Odysseus shrouds Polyxena and leads her out.*
> > *Hecuba collapses to the ground.*)

Hecuba
> I am faint—my legs give way beneath me—
> Polyxena!
>   Touch your mother, give me your hand,
> reach me! Do not leave me childless!
>   O gods,   440
> to see there, in her place, Helen of Sparta,
> sister of the sons of Zeus, whose lovely eyes
> made ashes of the happiness of Troy!

Chorus
> O wind of ocean,
> wind that blows on the sea
> and drives the scudding ships,   445
> where are you blowing me?
> Where shall I be slave?
> Where is there home for me?
> There in distant Doris,   450
> in Phthia far away

where men say Apidanus runs,
father of waters,
river whose lovely flowing
fattens the fields?

There in the islands?   455
The salt sea churning, borne on by oars,
to days of mourning in the house,
there where the primal palm
and the bay broke out their leaves
for lovely Leto   460
in honor of her son?
There shall I sing
with the maidens of Delos,
praising Artemis,
the bow and fillets of gold?   465

Or there where Athene drives
her chariot of burnished gold?
There in Athens, yoking
the horses on the goddess' robe,
stitching cloth of saffron
with threads of every color,   470
sewing the Titans there,
killed by stabbing fire,
the thunderbolts of Zeus?

O my children!   475
My father, my mother!
O city, ruined land,
ashes and smoke, wasted,
wilderness of war!
I live, but live a slave,   480
forced to a foreign land,
torn westward out of Asia
to a marriage that is death!

                                    (Enter Talthybius.)

Talthybius

Women of Troy, where can I find Hecuba,   485
your onetime queen?

Coryphaeus

There she lies, Talthybius,
in the dust at your feet, her head buried in her robes.

Talthybius

O Zeus, what can I say?
That you look on man
and care?
Or do we, holding that the gods exist,
deceive ourselves with unsubstantial dreams   490
and lies, while random careless chance and change
alone control the world?
This was the queen
of fabulous Troy. This was once the wife
of Priam the great.
And now, childless, old,   495
enslaved, her home and city wrecked by war,
she lies there on the ground, her proud head
fouled in the dust.
I too am old,
an old man, and life is precious now,
but I would rather die than sink as low
as this poor woman has fallen now.
Rise,
lady. Lift your head to the light; raise
that body blanched with age.   500

Hecuba

Who are you
who will not let me lie? Who disturbs
my wretchedness? Why?

Talthybius

I am Talthybius,
herald of the Greeks, lady. I bring you a message
from Agamemnon.

Hecuba

                           Have the Greeks decreed my death?   505
Tell me that, and you are welcome, herald.
No other news could please me now.

Talthybius

                                 No, not that.
I come on behalf of the army and the sons of Atreus   510
to bid you bury your daughter. She is dead.

Hecuba

Is that your news, herald?
                            I cannot die?
You came to tell me *this*?
                        O gods, my child!
My poor child! Torn from my arms! Dead!
Dead. All my children died with you.
How did you put her to death? With honor and respect,   515
or did you kill her savagely, with cold brutality?
Tell me. Let me hear it all, everything,
no matter how it hurts.

Talthybius

                       There is a cost
in telling too, a double price of tears,
for I was crying when your daughter died,
and I will cry again while telling you,   520
lady. But listen.
                  The whole army of the Greeks,
drawn up in ranks, was present at the execution,
waiting and watching while Polyxena was led
by Achilles' son slowly through the center of the camp
and up the tomb. I stood nearby, while behind her
came a troop of soldiers purposely appointed   525
to prevent her struggles.
                  Then Achilles' son
lifted a golden beaker to pour the offering

of wine to his father's ghost and nodded to me
to call for silence.

           "Quiet, Achaeans!" I shouted,   530
"Silence in the ranks!" and instantly a hush
fell upon the army and he began to pray:
"Great ghost of my father Achilles, receive
this offering I pour to charm your spirit up.   535
Rise and drink this gift we give to you,
this virgin's fresh blood. Be gracious to us:
set free our ships and loose our anchor-ropes.
Grant to us all our day of coming home,
grant us all to come home safe from Troy!"   540
So he prayed, and the army with him.

                        Then,
grasping his sword by its golden hilt, he slipped it
from the sheath, and made a sign to the soldiers
to seize her. But she spoke first:

                  "Wait, you Greeks   545
who sacked my city! Of my own free will I die.
Let no man touch me. I offer my throat
willingly to the sword. I will not flinch.
But let me be free for now. Let me die free.   550
I am of royal blood, and I scorn to die
the death of a slave."

               "Free her!" the army roared,
and Agamemnon ordered his men to let her go.
The instant they released their hold, she grasped her robes
at the shoulder and ripped them open down the sides   555
as far as the waist, exposing her naked breasts,
bare and lovely like a sculptured goddess.   560
Then she sank, kneeling on the ground, and spoke
her most heroic words:

                "Strike, captain.
Here is my breast. Will you stab me there?
Or in the neck? Here is my throat, bared   565
for your blow."

Torn between pity and duty,
Achilles' son stood hesitating, and then
slashed her throat with the edge of his sword. The blood
gushed out, and she fell, dying, to the ground,
but even as she dropped, managed to fall somehow
with grace, modestly hiding what should be hidden   570
from men's eyes.

The execution finished,
the soldiers set to work. Some scattered leaves
upon her corpse, while others brought branches
of pine and heaped her pyre. Those who shirked   575
found themselves abused by the rest.

"You loafers,"
they shouted, "how can you stand there empty-handed,
doing nothing? Where's your present for the girl?
When did you ever see greater courage
than that?"

And now you know it all.

For my part,   580
having seen your daughter die, I count you
of all women the one most blessed in her children
and also the unhappiest.

Coryphaeus

Blow after blow
disaster drops from heaven; suffering shakes
my city and the house of Priam.

Hecuba

O my child,
how shall I deal with this thronging crowd of blows,   585
these terrors, each with its petition, clamoring
for attention? If I try to cope with one,
another shoulders in, and then a third
comes on, distracting, each fresh wave
breeding new successors as it breaks.

But now,
with this last blow I cannot cope at all,

cannot forget your death, cannot stop   590
crying—
        And yet a kind of comfort comes
in knowing how well you died.
                    But how strange it seems.
Even worthless ground, given a gentle push
from heaven, will harvest well, while fertile soil,
starved of what it needs, bears badly.   595
But human nature never seems to change;
evil stays itself, evil to the end,
and goodness good, its nature uncorrupted
by any shock or blow, always the same,
enduring excellence.
            Is it in our blood
or something we acquire? But goodness can be taught,   600
and any man who knows what goodness is
knows evil too, because he judges
from the good.
         But all this is the rambling nothing
of despair.
        Talthybius, go to the Greeks
and tell them this from me: not a hand
is to be laid on my child; make them keep   605
the crowd away.
           For in armies the size of this,
men are prone to violence, sailors undisciplined,
the mob gets out of hand, runs wild, worse
than raging fire, while the man who stands apart
is called a coward.
            (*Exit Talthybius. Hecuba turns to a Handmaid.*)
         —Take your pitcher, old woman,
fill it with water from the sea and then return.   610
I must give my daughter's body its last bath
before her burial, this wedding which is death.
For she marries Hades, and I must bathe the bride
and lay her out as she deserves.

But how?
I have nothing of my own, nothing precious left.
What then?
                    I'll borrow from my women in the tents   615
those few poor trinkets they managed to pilfer
from their own homes.

                                        (*Exit Handmaid.*)
                    Where is greatness gone?
Where is it now, that stately house, home
where I was happy once? King Priam,
blessed with children once, in your pride of wealth?   620
And what am I of all I used to be,
mother of sons, mother of princes?
                                        Gone,
all gone, and nothing left.
                    And yet
we boast, are proud, we plume our confidence—
the rich man in his insolence of wealth,
the public man's conceit of office or success—   625
and we are nothing; our ambition, greatness, pride,
all vanity.
                    That man is happiest
who lives from day to day and asks no more,
garnering the simple goodness of a life.

                                        (*Hecuba enters the tent.*)
Chorus
        That morning was my fate,
        that hour doom was done,   630
        when Paris felled the tree
        that grew on Ida's height
        and made a ship for sea
        and sailed to Helen's bed—
        loveliest of women   635
        the golden sun has seen.

Grief, and worse than grief,
necessity surrounds us.
One man's folly made
a universal curse, 640
ruin over Simois.
Paris sat as judge
upon three goddesses. 645
His verdict was war.

War, slaughter, and the ruin of my house,
while in her house the Spartan woman mourns,
grieving by the wide Eurotas, 650
and mothers mourn for their sons,
and tear out their snowy hair
and dredge their cheeks with bloody nails. 655

(*The Handmaid rushes in.*)

Handmaid
Where is the queen, women?
Where is Hecuba
whose sufferings outstrip all rival runners?
No one shall take that crown away. 660

Coryphaeus
Speak.
What new sorrow do you bring her? Will this news
of anguish never sleep?

(*Enter other women, carrying on a bier the
shrouded corpse of Polydorus.*)

Handmaid
This is the grief
I bring to Hecuba. Gentle words are hard
to find: the burden I bring is disaster.

(*Enter Hecuba from the tent.*)

Coryphaeus
Look: here she comes now. 665

Handmaid
O my queen,
more wretched, more miserable than I can say.
Now you live no more, the light is gone!

Hecuba

    This is mockery, not news. I know it all.   670
    But why have you brought Polyxena's body here?
    I heard the Greeks were helping with her funeral.

Handmaid

    Poor woman, she thinks it is Polyxena.
    She does not know the worst.   675

Hecuba

                O gods, *no*!
    Not my poor mad daughter, Cassandra?

Handmaid

    Cassandra is alive. Mourn for this dead boy.
                (She strips the shroud from the corpse.)
    Look at this naked corpse we found,
    this unexpected horror.   680

Hecuba

              It is my son!
    Polydorus, warded by my friend in Thrace!
    No!

        O gods in heaven, let me die!

        O my son, my son,
        now the awful dirge begins,   685
        the fiend, the fury,
        singing, wailing in me now,
        shrieking madness!

Handmaid

    What fury? Is it the curse of Paris you mean?

Hecuba

    Horror too sudden to be believed,
        unbelievable loss,
        blow after blow!   690
    And this is all my life:
        the mourning endless,
        the anguish unending.

Coryphaeus
In loss and suffering we live our lives.

Hecuba
  O my son, my child,   695
  how were you killed?
  What fate, what hand
  could take your life?

Handmaid
I do not know. I found his body lying
on the shore.

Hecuba
      Drowned, his body washed on the sand? 700
  Or was he murdered?

Handmaid
        The surf had washed his body up.

Hecuba
  O gods, my dream!
        I see it now,
  those black wings beating the dark,   705
  brushing over him, touching him,
  dead already, even in my dreams!

Coryphaeus
Who murdered him? Did your dream show you that?

Hecuba
  Who but our noble friend in Thrace,   710
  where his father sent him out of harm,
  to be safe with our friend in Thrace?

Coryphaeus
Murdered? Murdered by a friend? Killed for gold?

Hecuba
  Unspeakable, unimaginable crime,
  unbearable!
      Where is friendship now?   715
  O fiend, monster, so pitiless,

to mangle him so, to hack
his sweet flesh with the sword!   720

Coryphaeus
   Unhappy Hecuba, most miserable of women
   on this earth, how heavily god's anger
   falls on you.
                 —But look: I see our master,
   Agamemnon, coming here.
                          Quickly, friends,   725
   withdraw.
                          (Enter Agamemnon with attendants.)

Agamemnon
              Why this delay of yours, Hecuba,
   in burying your daughter? I received your message
   from Talthybius that none of our men should touch her,
   and I gave strict orders to that effect.
   Hence I found your delay all the more surprising   730
   and came to fetch you myself. In any case,
   I can report that matters there are well in hand
   and proceeding nicely—if a word like "nicely"
   has any meaning in this connection.

                          (He sees the corpse of Polydorus.)
                          Here,
   what's that Trojan corpse beside the tents?
   I can see from his shroud that he's not a Greek.   735

Hecuba (aside)
   O gods, what shall I do?
                          Throw myself
   at his knees and beg for mercy or hold my tongue
   and suffer in silence?

Agamemnon
                          Why do you turn away,
   Hecuba? And what's the meaning of these tears?
   What happened here? Who is this man?   740

Hecuba (aside)
But suppose he treats me with contempt, like a slave,
and pushes me away? I could not bear it.

Agamemnon
I am not a prophet, Hecuba. Unless you speak,
you make it quite impossible for me to help you.

Hecuba (aside)
And yet I could be wrong. Am I imagining? 745
He may mean well.

Agamemnon
                    If you have nothing to say,
Hecuba, very well. I have no wish to hear.

Hecuba (aside)
But without his help I lose my only chance
of revenging my children. So why should I hesitate? 750
Win or lose, he is my only hope.

                              (*She falls at Agamemnon's knees.*)
Agamemnon, I implore you, I beg you
by your beard, your knees, by this conquering hand, help me!

Agamemnon
What can I do to help you, Hecuba? Your freedom
is yours for the asking.

Hecuba
                    No, not freedom. 755
Revenge. Only give me my revenge
and I'll gladly stay a slave the rest of my life.

Agamemnon
Revenge? Revenge on whom, Hecuba?

Hecuba
                              My lord,
not the revenge you think, not that at all.
Do you see this body here, this naked corpse 760
for which I mourn?

Agamemnon
> I see him very well,
though no one yet has told me who he is.

Hecuba
This was my son. I gave him birth.

Agamemnon
> Which son,
poor woman?

Hecuba
> Not one of those who died
for Troy.

Agamemnon
> You mean you had another son?   765

Hecuba
Another son to die. This was he.

Agamemnon
But where was he living when Troy was taken?

Hecuba
His father sent him away to save his life.

Agamemnon
This was the only son he sent away?
Where did he send him?

Hecuba
> Here. To this country
where his body was found.

Agamemnon
> He sent him to Polymestor,   770
the king of Thrace?

Hecuba
> And with his son he also sent
a sum of fatal gold.

Agamemnon
But how did he die? Who killed him?

Hecuba

Who else?
His loving host, our loyal friend in Thrace.

Agamemnon

Then his motive, you think, was the gold?   775

Hecuba

Yes.
The instant he heard that Troy had fallen, he killed.

Agamemnon

But where was the body found? Who brought him here?

Hecuba

This old servant here. She found his body
lying on the beach.

Agamemnon

What was she doing there?
Searching?

Hecuba

No. She went to fetch water
for Polyxena's burial.

Agamemnon

He must have killed him first,   780
then thrown his body in the sea.

Hecuba

Hacked him, tossed him
to the pounding surf.

Agamemnon

I pity you, Hecuba.
Your suffering has no end.

Hecuba

I died
long ago. Nothing can touch me now.

Agamemnon

What woman on this earth was ever cursed   785
like this?

Hecuba
> There is none but goddess Suffering
herself.
> But let me tell you why I kneel
at your feet. And if my sufferings seem just,
then I must be content. But if otherwise,
give me my revenge on that treacherous friend   790
who flouted every god in heaven and in hell
to do this brutal murder.
> At our table
he was our frequent guest; was counted first
among our friends, respected, honored by me,
receiving every kindness that a man could meet—   795
and then, in cold deliberation, killed
my son.
> Murder may have its reasons, its motives,
but this—to refuse my son a grave, to throw him
to the sea, unburied!
> I am a slave, I know,
and slaves are weak. But the gods are strong, and over them
there stands some absolute, some moral order   800
or principle of law more final still.
Upon this moral law the world depends;
through it the gods exist; by it we live,
defining good and evil.
> Apply that law
to me. For if you flout it now, and those
who murder in cold blood or defy the gods
go unpunished, then human justice withers,   805
corrupted at its source.
> Honor my request,
Agamemnon.
> Punish this murder.
> Pity me.
Be like a painter. Stand back, see me
in perspective,

see me whole, observe
my wretchedness—
               once a queen, and now
a slave; blessed with children, happy once,   810
now old, childless, utterly alone,
homeless, lost, unhappiest of women
on this earth. . . .

                           (*Agamemnon turns away.*)
           O gods, you turn away—
what can I do? My only hope is lost.
O this helplessness!
              Why, why
do we make so much of knowledge, struggle so hard   815
to get some little skill not worth the effort?
But persuasion, the only art whose power
is absolute, worth any price we pay,
we totally neglect. And so we fail;
we lose our hopes.
            But as for happiness,
who could look at me and any longer   820
dare to hope:
            I have seen my children die,
and bound to shame I walk this homeless earth,
a slave, and see the smoke that leaps up
over Troy.
          It may be futile now
to urge the claims of love, but let me urge them   825
anyway. At your side sleeps my daughter
Cassandra, once the priestess of Apollo.
What will you give, my lord, for those nights of love?
What thanks for all her tenderness in bed
does she receive from you, and I, in turn,   830
from her?
         Look now at this dead boy,
Cassandra's brother. Revenge him. Be kind to her
by being kind to him.

One word more.   835
If by some magic, some gift of the gods,
I could become all speech—tongues in my arms,
hands that talked, voices speaking, crying
from my hair and feet—then, all together,
as one voice, I would fall and touch your knees,
crying, begging, imploring with a thousand tongues—   840
O master, greatest light of Hellas,
hear me,
        help an old woman,
                        avenge her!
She is nothing at all, but hear her, help her
even so. Do your duty as a man of honor:
see justice done. Punish this murder.   845

Coryphaeus

How strange in their reversals are our lives.
Necessities define us all, as now,
joining enemies in common cause
and alienating friends.

Agamemnon

                I pity you deeply,
Hecuba, for the tragic death of this poor boy.   850
And I am touched and stirred by your request.
So far as justice is concerned, god knows,
nothing would please me more than to bring
this murderer to book.
                        But my position
here is delicate. If I give you your revenge,
the army is sure to charge that I connived   855
at the death of the king of Thrace because of my love
for Cassandra. This is my dilemma. The army
thinks of Polymestor as its friend,
this boy as its enemy. You love your son,
but what do your affections matter to the Greeks?   860
Put yourself in my position.

Believe me,
Hecuba, I should like to act on your behalf
and would come instantly to your defense.
But if the army mutters, then I must
be slow.

Hecuba

Then no man on earth is truly free.   865
All are slaves of money or necessity.
Public opinion or fear of prosecution
forces each one, against his conscience,
to conform.

But since your fears make you defer
to the mob, let a slave set you free
from what you fear.

Be my confidant,   870
the silent partner of my plot to kill my son's
murderer. Give me your passive support.
Then if violence breaks out or the Greeks
attempt a rescue, obstruct them covertly
without appearing to act for me.

For the rest,   875
have no fear. I shall manage.

Agamemnon

How?
Poison? Or do you think that shaking hand
could lift a sword and kill? Who would help you?
On whom could you count?

Hecuba

Remember: there are women   880
hidden in these tents.

Agamemnon

You mean our prisoners?

Hecuba

They will help me get revenge.

Agamemnon
                        But *women?*
    Women overpower men?

Hecuba
                    There is power
in numbers, and cunning makes us strong.

Agamemnon
                        True,   885
    though I admit to being skeptical of women
    in a matter like this.

Hecuba
                Why?
                    Women killed
Aegyptus' sons. Women emptied Lemnos
of its males: we murdered every one. And so
it shall be here.
                But of that I say no more.
Let this woman have your safe-conduct
through the army.

            (*Agamemnon nods. Hecuba turns to the Handmaid.*)
                Go to Polymestor
and give him this message:
                    "Hecuba, once queen of Troy,   890
summons you on business that concerns you both
and requests you bring your sons. They also share
in what she has to say."

                (*Exit Handmaid with several attendants.*)
                One more favor,
Agamemnon.
                Defer my daughter's funeral   895
until my son's body is placed beside her
on the pyre. Let them burn together,
brother and sister joined in a single flame,
their mother's double grief.

Agamemnon

As you wish.
If we could sail, I could not grant this. But now,
until heaven sends us a favoring wind,   900
we must ride at anchor here.

I wish you luck
in your attempt.

The common interests
of states and individuals alike demand
that good and evil receive their just rewards.

(*Exit Agamemnon, followed by attendants. Hecuba and
her women withdraw into the tent with the
body of Polydorus.*)

Chorus

O Ilium! O my country,   905
whose name men speak no more
among unfallen cities!
So dense a cloud of Greeks
came, spear on spear, destroying!
Your crown of towers shorn away,   910
and everywhere the staining fire,
most pitiful. O Ilium,
whose ways I shall not walk again!

At midnight came my doom.
Midnight when the feast is done
and sleep falls sweetly on the eyes.   915
The songs and sacrifice,
the dances, all were done.
My husband lay asleep,
his spear upon the wall,   920
forgetting for a while
the ships drawn up on Ilium's shore.

I was setting my hair
in the soft folds of the net,
gazing at the endless light

deep in the golden mirror,   925
preparing myself for bed,
when tumult broke the air
and shouts and cries
shattered the empty streets:—
Onward, onward, you Greeks!   930
Sack the city of Troy
and see your homes once more!

Dressed only in a gown
like a girl of Sparta,
I left the bed of love
and prayed to Artemis.   935
But no answer came.
I saw my husband lying dead,
and they took me over sea.
Backward I looked at Troy,
but the ship sped on
and Ilium slipped away,   940
and I was dumb with grief.

A curse on Helen,
sister of the sons of Zeus,
and my curse on him,
disastrous Paris   945
whose wedding wasted Troy!
O adulterous marriage!
Helen, fury of ruin!   950
Let the wind blow
and never bring her home!
Let there be no landing
for Helen of Troy!

(*Enter Polymestor, followed by his two young sons and several*
attendants. Throughout his speech, Hecuba refuses to rec-
ognize him, keeping her back turned and her
eyes fixed on the ground.)

Polymestor

Dearest Hecuba, wife of my dear friend,
poor unhappy Priam!

How I pity you,
you and your ruined Troy. And now this latest blow,   955
your daughter's death. . . .

What can we take on trust
in this uncertain life? Happiness, greatness,
pride—nothing is secure, nothing keeps.
The inconsistent gods make chaos of our lives,
pitching us about with such savagery of change
that we, out of our anguish and uncertainty,
may turn to them.

—But how does my sorrow help?   960
Your loss remains.

(*A short silence, while Polymestor waits for Hecuba to recognize him. When she does not, he continues with mounting embarrassment.*)

But perhaps you are angry with me, Hecuba,
for not coming to you earlier. If so, forgive me.
It just so happened that I was inland, in the mountains
of Thrace, at the time when you arrived. In fact,
I was on the point of coming here myself   965
when your servant arrived and gave me your message.
Needless to say, I lost no time.

Hecuba

Polymestor,
I am so embarrassed by the state in which you see me,
fallen so low since when you saw me last,
I cannot look you in the face.

Forgive it,   970
and do not think me rude, Polymestor.
In any case, habit and custom excuse me,
forbidding that a woman look directly at a man.   975

Polymestor

   I quite understand.

                        Now, how can I help you?

   You sent for me on some business, I believe?

Hecuba

   I have a matter to discuss with you and your sons.

   But privately, if possible.

                          Could you ask your men   980

   to withdraw?

Polymestor

                               (*To his bodyguard.*)

        You may leave. There is no danger here.

   This woman is my friend and the army of the Greeks

   is well disposed.

                 Now, Hecuba, to business.

   How can I, your prosperous friend, help you   985

   in your time of troubles?

Hecuba

                   One question first.

   How is my son Polydorus, your ward?

   Is he alive?

            Anything else can wait.

Polymestor

   Alive and well. In this respect at least,

   you may put your mind at rest.

Hecuba

                  My dearest friend,   990

   how like you your kindness is!

Polymestor

              What else

   would give you comfort?

Hecuba

             Does he still remember his mother?

Polymestor
So much that he wanted to run away
and visit you in secret.

Hecuba

And the gold from Troy?
Is it safe?

Polymestor

Quite safe. Locked in my palace   995
under strong guard.

Hecuba

Guard it well, my friend.
Do not let it tempt you.

Polymestor

Have no fears.
What I have of my own is quite enough
to last my life.

Hecuba

Do you know why I sent for you
and your sons?

Polymestor

Not yet. We are waiting to hear.

Hecuba
You are my friend, a friend for whom I feel   1000
no less love than you have shown to me.
And my business concerns—

Polymestor

Yes? Yes? Go on.

Hecuba
—the ancient vaults, the gold of Priam's house.

Polymestor
I am to pass this information to your son?

Hecuba
In person. I know you for a man of honor.

Polymestor

But why did you ask that my sons be present?   1005

Hecuba

I thought they should know. Something, for instance,
might happen to you.

Polymestor

                    A prudent precaution.
    I quite agree.

Hecuba

                Do you know where Athene's temple
    once stood in Troy?

Polymestor

                    The gold is there?
    Is there a marker?

Hecuba

                    A black rock jutting up   1010
    above the ground.

Polymestor

                Is that all?

Hecuba

                        No:
    my jewels. I smuggled some jewels away from Troy.
    Could you keep them for me?

Polymestor

                        You have them with you?
    Where are they hidden?

Hecuba

                    There, inside the tent,
    beneath a heap of spoils.

Polymestor

                    Inside the tent?   1015
    Here, in the Greek camp?

Hecuba

                    The women's quarters
    are separate from the main camp.

Polymestor
                                    Is it safe?
    Are there men around?

Hecuba
                        No men; only women.
But come inside. We have no time to lose.
Quick.
            The Greek army is waiting and eager   1020
to raise their anchors and sail for home.
                                    Then,
when our business here is done, you may go
and take your children where you left my son.

                    (*Polymestor and his sons, followed by Hecuba,
                                        enter the tent.*)

Coryphaeus
    Death is the debt of life. Now your debt falls due:—

Chorus (*individually*)
    —As though you stumbled in the surf   1025

    —hurled from high ambition down

    —trapped, thrashing with terror
      in the swirling tow

    —   and the water
      closing overhead

    —   until
      you drown.

    —   And now you know:

    —Life is held on loan.

    —The price of life is death.

    —Those who take a life—

    —repay it with their own.

    —Justice and the gods   1030
      exact the loan at last.

    —Gleam of gold misled you.

—You took the final turn

—where the bitter road veers off

—and runs downhill

—   to death!

—Hands which never held a sword

—shall wrench your twisted life away!

> *(Sudden screams and commotion from inside the tent.)*

Polymestor *(from within)*
Blind! Blind!
        O light!
                Light of my eyes!   1035

Coryphaeus
That scream of anguish! Did you hear that scream?

Polymestor *(from within)*
                                Help!

Look out, children!
                Murder!
                        Run! Murder!

Coryphaeus
New murder, fresh horror in the tent!

> *(More screams and uproar; then a sudden furious batter-*
> *tering on the walls of the tent.)*

Polymestor *(from within)*
Run, damn you, run!
                But I'll get you yet!
I'll batter down this tent with my bare fists!   1040

Chorus *(individually)*
—Listen to him hammer at the walls!

—What should we do?

—   Break down the door
—Hurry!

—   Hecuba needs our help!

> *(Hecuba emerges from the tent.)*

Hecuba

Pound away!

Go on, batter down the door!

Nothing in this world can ever give you back   1045

the light of your eyes. Nothing.

Never again

shall you see your sons, see them alive.

I have killed your sons, and you are blind!

Coryphaeus

Have you done it? Have you done this thing you say?

Hecuba

Be patient a moment, and then see for yourself.

Watch him as he stumbles and staggers out of the tent—   1050

stone-blind.

See the bodies of his sons,

killed by my women and me.

His debt is paid

and I have my revenge.

But hush: here he comes,

raging from the tent. Let me keep out of his reach.

In his fury he will stop at nothing now.   1055

(*Polymestor, blood pouring from his eyes, emerges from the tent
on all fours. Wildly and blindly he scrambles about like an
animal, searching for the women with his hands.*)

Polymestor

Where?

Where shall I run?

Where shall I stop?

Where?

Like a raging beast I go,

running on all fours

to track my quarry down!

Where?

Where?

Here?

Where?   1060

Where can I pounce
on those murderous hags of Troy?
Where are you, women?
Where are they hiding,
those bitches of Troy? 1065

O god of the sun,
heal these bleeding eyes!
Give me back the light of my eyes!
Shh.
      The sound of footsteps. 1070
But where?
         Where can I leap?
Gods, to gorge their blood,
to rip the living flesh,
feed like a starving beast,
blood for blood!
         No, no. 1075
Where am I running now?
My children abandoned,
left for Furies to claw,
for savage bitches to gorge,
their mangled bodies thrown
to whiten on the hill!
But where?
         Where shall I run?
Where can I stand at bay? 1080
Run, run, run,
gather robes and run!
Let me run for my lair,
run like a ship,
sails furled, for the shore!
I'll run for my lair
and stand at bay
where my children are!

(He rushes into the tent and comes out carrying the bodies of
his children. He lays them down and crouches
over them protectively.)

« 57 »

Coryphaeus

Tormented man! Tortured past enduring.   1085
You suffer now as you made others suffer.

Polymestor

Help me, you men of Thrace!
Help!
      Soldiers, horsemen,
help! Come with spears!   1090
Achaeans, help! Help me,
sons of Atreus!
        Help!
           Help!
Hear me, help me, help!
Where are you?
        Help me.
Women have killed my sons.   1095
Murder, dreadful murder!
Butchery! Horror!
Help me!
     Help!
        O gods,
where can I go?
Where can I run?
You gods in heaven,
give me wings to fly!   1100
Let me leap to heaven
where the vaulted stars,
Sirius and Orion,
flare out their fire,
or plunge to Hades
on the blackened flood!   1105

Coryphaeus

Who could reproach this man for wanting to die?
Death is what men want when the anguish of living
is more than they can bear.

                  (Enter Agamemnon, attended by soldiers.)

Agamemnon
                        Shouting and screams
of terror brought me here. Ringing Echo,
born of these mountain crags, resounded the cries,   1110
shunting them back and forth throughout the camp,
alarming the men. Unless we knew for a fact
that Troy had fallen to our arms, this uproar
could have caused no little terror or disturbance.

Polymestor
That voice! I know it.
                        —My friend, Agamemnon!
Look, look at me now—

Agamemnon
                        Oh. Awful sight!   1115
Poor Polymestor! Those blind bleeding eyes,
those dead children. . . . Who did this, Polymestor?
Who killed these boys? Who put out your eyes?
Whoever it was, he must have hated you and your sons
with a savage, ruthless hate.

Polymestor
                        Hecuba. She did it,   1120
she and the other women. They destroyed me,
they worse than destroyed me.

Agamemnon
                        You, Hecuba?
Do you admit this hideous, inhuman crime?   1125
Is this atrocity your work?

Polymestor
                        Hecuba?
Is *she* here?
                Where? Tell me where she is,
and I'll claw her to pieces with these bare hands!

Agamemnon
                                (*Forcibly restraining him.*)
What? Have you lost your mind?

Polymestor
> For god's sake,
let me go! Let me rip her limb from limb!

Agamemnon
Stop.
> No more of this inhuman savagery now.
Each of you will give his version of the case   1130
and I shall try to judge you both impartially.

Polymestor
Then listen, Agamemnon.
> Hecuba had a son
called Polydorus, her youngest. His father Priam,
apprehensive that Troy would shortly be taken,   1135
sent the boy to me to be raised in my own house.
I killed him, and I admit it.
> My action, however,
was dictated, as you shall see, by a policy
of wise precaution.
> My primary motive was fear,
fear that if this boy, your enemy, survived,
he might someday found a second and resurgent Troy.
Further, when the Greeks heard that Priam's son   1140
was still alive, I feared that they would raise
a second expedition against this new Troy,
in which case these fertile plains of Thrace
would once again be ravaged by war; once again
Troy and her troubles would work her neighbors harm—
those same hardships, my lord, which we in Thrace
have suffered in this war.
> Hecuba, however,   1145
somehow hearing that her son was dead or murdered,
lured me here on the pretext of revealing
the secret hiding-place of Priam's gold
in Troy. Then, alleging that we might be overheard,
she led my sons and me, unattended,
into the tent.

Surrounded by Trojan women
on every side, I took my seat on a couch.   1150
The atmosphere seemed one of friendliness.
The women fingered my robes, then lifted the cloth
to inspect it under the light, exclaiming shrilly
over the quality of our Thracian weaving.
Still others stood there admiring my lance   1155
and before I knew it I was stripped of spear
and shield alike.
        Meanwhile the young mothers
were fussing over my children, jouncing them in their arms
with hugs and kisses and passing them from hand to hand
until they were out of reach.
             Then, incredibly,
out of that scene of domestic peace,   1160
they suddenly pulled daggers from their robes
and butchered both my sons, while troops of women
rushed to tackle me, seizing my arms and legs
and holding me down. I tried to leap up   1165
but they caught me by the hair and pulled me down.
I fought to free my arms, but they swamped me
and I went down beneath a flood of women,
unable to move a muscle.
           And then—O gods!—
they crowned their hideous work with worse outrage,
the most inhuman brutal crime of all.
They lifted their brooches and stabbed these bleeding eyes   1170
through and through! Then they ran for cover,
scattering through the tent. I leaped to my feet,
groping along the wall, stalking them down
like a wounded animal hunting a pack of hounds,
staggering blind on all fours, battering   1175
at the wall.
        This is my reward, Agamemnon,
for my efforts in disposing of your enemies.
What I suffer now I suffer for you.
One word more.

On behalf of all those dead
who learned their hatred of women long ago,
for those who hate them now, for those unborn
who shall live to hate them yet, I now declare   1180
my firm conviction:
                        neither earth nor ocean
produces a creature as savage and monstrous
as woman.
            This is my experience.
I know that this is true.

Coryphaeus

                        Do not presume,
Polymestor, whatever your provocation,
to include all women in this sweeping curse   1185
without distinction.

Hecuba

                        The clear actions of a man,
Agamemnon, should speak louder than any words.
Good words should get their goodness from our lives
and nowhere else; the evil we do should show,
a rottenness that festers in our speech   1190
and what we say, incapable of being glozed
with a film of pretty words.
                            There are men, I know,
sophists who make a science of persuasion,
glozing evil with the slick of loveliness;
but in the end a speciousness will show.
The impostors are punished; not one escapes
his death.
            So much by way of beginning.   1195
Now for him.
            He claims he killed my son
on your behalf, Agamemnon, to spare
you Greeks the horrors of a second war.

                        (*She turns to Polymestor.*)

You liar!

First, what possible friendship could there be
between civilized Greeks and half-savages   1200
like you?

      Clearly none.

               Then why this zeal
to serve their cause?

              Are you related to them
or bound by marriage?

              What *is* your motive then?
Fear, you say, that they might sail for Troy
and burn your crops or ravage your kingdom in passing.
Who could believe that preposterous lie?

                    No,   1205
if you want the truth, let me tell you why:
it was your greed for gold that killed my son,
sheer greed and nothing more.

              If not,
what explains your conduct then and now?
Answer me this.

        Why, when Troy still flourished,
when the ramparts ran unbroken about the city,
when Priam was alive and Hector had his day—   1210
why, if you were then so friendly to the Greeks,
did you fail to kill my son or take him prisoner
at least, when you had him at your mercy?

                 But no.
You waited, biding your time, until our sun
had set, and the smoke announced the sack of Troy.   1215
Then you moved, killing your guest who sat
helpless at your hearth.

           And what of this,
which shows your crime for what it was?

                  Why,
if you loved the Greeks as much as you assert,
did you miss your chance to present them with the gold—   1220

that gold you claim does not belong to you
but to Agamemnon? But they were desperate then,
long years away from home.

But no. Even now
you cannot bear the thought of giving up
the gold, but hoard it for yourself at home.
One point more.

If you had done your duty
by my son, raised him and kept him safe,   1225
men would honor and respect you as a noble friend.
For real friendship is shown in times of trouble;
prosperity is full of friends.

And then,
if someday you had stood in need of help,
my son would have been your friend and treasury.
But killing him you killed your loyal friend;   1230
your gold is worthless now, your sons are dead,
and you are as you are.

(*She turns back to Agamemnon.*)

Agamemnon,
if you acquit this man, you prove yourself
unjust.

This is a man who betrayed his trust,
who killed against the laws of man and god,
faithless, evil, corrupt.

Acquit him now   1235
and we shall say the same is true of you.
I say no more.

Coryphaeus

Well spoken, Hecuba.
Those whose cause is just will never lack
good arguments.

Agamemnon

It gives me no pleasure   1240
to sit as judge on the miseries of others.

« 64 »

But I should cut a sorry figure in the world
if I allowed this case to come to court
and then refused or failed to give a verdict.
I have no choice.

             Know then, Polymestor,
I find you guilty of murder as charged.
You murdered your ward, killed him in cold blood,
and not, as you assert, for the Greeks or me,
but out of simple greed, to get his gold.   1245
You then construed the facts to fit your case
in court.

        Perhaps you think it a trifling matter
to kill a guest.

           We Greeks call it murder.
How, therefore, could I acquit you now
without losing face among men?

                   I could not do it.   1250
You committed a brutal crime; therefore accept
the consequences of your act.

Polymestor

              O gods,
condemned! Defeated by a woman, by a slave!

Hecuba

Condemned for what you did. Justly condemned.

Polymestor

O my children!

           O light, light of my eyes!   1255

Hecuba

It hurts, does it? And what of me? I mourn
my children too.

Polymestor

             Does it give you pleasure
to mock at me?

Hecuba

           I rejoice in my revenge.

Polymestor
Enjoy it now. You shall not enjoy it long.
Hear my prediction.
                    I foretell that you—

Hecuba
Shall be carried on ship across the sea to Hellas?   1260

Polymestor
—*shall drown at sea. You shall climb to the masthead
and fall—*

Hecuba
                    Pushed by force?

Polymestor
                                        *You shall climb the mast
of your own free will—*

Hecuba
                    Climb the mast? With wings?

Polymestor
—*changed to a dog, a bitch with blazing eyes.*   1265

Hecuba
How could you know of this transformation?

Polymestor
Because our Thracian prophet, Dionysus,
told me so.

Hecuba
                    He neglected, I see, to foretell
your own fate.

Polymestor
                    Had he told my future then,
I never would have stumbled in your trap.

Hecuba
Shall I live or die?

Polymestor
                    Die. And when you die   1270
your tomb shall be called—

Hecuba

In memory of my change?

Polymestor
—*Cynossema, the bitch's grave, a landmark
to sailors.*

Hecuba

What do I care how I die?
I have my revenge.

Polymestor

And your daughter Cassandra   1275

must also die—

Hecuba

I spit your prophecies back.
Use them on yourself.

Polymestor

(*Pointing to Agamemnon.*)
—*killed by this man's wife,
cut down by the bitter keeper of his house.*

Hecuba

Clytemnestra? She would never do it.

Polymestor
*Then she shall lift the dripping axe once more
and kill her husband too.*

Agamemnon

Are you out of your head?
Are you asking for more trouble?

Polymestor

Kill me,   1280

but a bath of blood waits for you in Argos.

Agamemnon

Slaves, carry him off! Drag him away!

(*Servants seize Polymestor.*)

Polymestor
Have I touched you now?

Agamemnon

Stop him. Gag his mouth.

Polymestor

Gag me. I have spoken.

Agamemnon

Take him away

this instant.

Then throw him on some desert island   1285

since his tongue cannot stop its impudence.

(*Attendants leave with Polymestor.*)

As for you, Hecuba, go now and bury

your two dead children.

The rest of you women,

go and report at once to your masters' tents.

For now the sudden wind sits freshly in our sails.   1290

May heaven grant that our ordeal is done

at last!

May all be well at home in Argos!

(*Exit Agamemnon with remaining attendants. Hecuba and her
women go slowly to the tent, leaving the stage empty except
for the abandoned bodies of Polymestor's sons.
The Chorus files slowly out.*)

Chorus

File to the tents,

file to the harbor.

There we embark

on life as slaves.

Necessity is harsh.   1295

Fate has no reprieve.

ANDROMACHE

Translated by John Frederick Nims

INTRODUCTION TO *ANDROMACHE*

Euripides' *Andromache* was written in the first years of the Peloponnesian War, probably between 430 and 424 B.C.; if inspired by a particular Spartan atrocity, the most likely would have been the massacre of the Plataean prisoners in 427. The scholiast reports that the play was not presented at Athens; it may have been performed at Argos (if at all) as part of an Athenian propaganda campaign, or at Epirus, where the young king, educated in Athens, was of the Molossian line acclaimed in the epilogue.

The discontinuity of the plot because of Andromache's disappearance in mid-play has troubled critics; not all have been as candid as D. W. Lucas, for whom the play "falls feebly and mysteriously to pieces. . . . there must be missing clues which would show the play less inept than it seems." (Professor Lucas comes up with a deadpan diagnosis worthy of Euripides himself: the poet, in these difficult days of plague and Spartan incursions, was temporarily out of his head.)

Verrall probably stands alone in defending the plot as such; he assumes (it seems wrongly) that the play is a sequel about a Machiavellian scheme concocted by Menelaus and Orestes. His theory "explains" the apparent breakdown of Menelaus in the presence of Peleus and does away with the time lapse during the chorus (ll. 1009–46), but it depends on effects that only an audience of well-briefed Verrallians could be expected to catch and relate. The breakdown of Menelaus needs no theory to explain it: Euripides' Spartan is a blusterer cowed by any show of vigor. The time lapse (of perhaps a week) is one of several in the extant tragedies; little is gained by pretending it is not there. In the excitement of the performance, who in the audience would be thinking in terms of mileages and time schedules? Who would even notice that the Chorus had been rather casual in informing Peleus of the intended murder of his grandson?

Some have suggested that Euripides, fascinated by character, is indifferent to plot. Once Andromache is out of danger, Euripides dismisses her to concentrate on her lively rival, much as Shakespeare scuttles the Turkish fleet when he has no further need for it.

Still others have found the unity of the play in *dianoia*. In antiquity it was already felt that Euripides often wrote what the poet and not what the plot demanded: Lucan said that "quite without dramatic necessity [Euripides] freely expressed his own opinions." In the words of a twentieth-century observer he "inserts passages suggested as much by the contemporary as by the dramatic situation." For *Andromache*, several key ideas have been proposed: it is about the house of Peleus—unsophisticated northerners undone by a southern alliance; or about the dangers to family life inherent in the practice of slaveholding; or it warns against incautious marriages; or it gives the *aition* of the tomb-worship of Peleus and Thetis; or it records a burning detestation of Sparta and Spartan ways.

Probably a more meaningful approach is that suggested independently by L. H. G. Greenwood and Gunther Zuntz. Euripides, says Greenwood, "is fond of presenting the arguments for or against this or that proposition concerning matters that were the subject of active interest and controversy. . . . he presents these arguments so impartially, and refrains so completely from pronouncing judgement . . . that we really cannot tell what he himself thinks." Zuntz reminds us of the problem of the Euripidean age: How is man to live in a godless world? "Different individuals had different answers, and Euripides gives them all."

It is helpful to keep in mind the philosophical background of the period: the irreconcilable systems of the pre-Socratics had led to the skepticism of the Sophists; if no one way of interpreting reality could be established as the right way, then any way was probably as good as any other. We cannot read long in Euripides before becoming aware of the doctrinal atomism of the age—an age whose values, says Jaeger, were rotten with individualism.

The conviction that standards were what the individual chose to make them was intensified by the war itself. Thucydides (iii. 10) gives a disturbing analysis of how even "words had to change their ordinary meaning and take that which was now given them." This in addition to the moral chaos of the plague of 430 B.C. (cf. ii. 7) which Euripides had lived through not long before he wrote *Andromache.*

It was an age that reminds us in many ways of the similarly disturbed world of the Jacobeans, filled, as Eliot says, with broken fragments of systems. "We have seene the best of our time," Gloucester desponds. "Machinations, hollownesse, treacherie, and all ruinous disorders follow us disquietly to our Graves." Perhaps John Webster has described it most poignantly, with his characters "in a miste" as they face the moment of truth, torn between the religious values of the past and the new self-interest for which Machiavelli was made the lurid figurehead.

In that environment, a restless and passionate temperament might well have been contemptuous of the Aristotelian dramatic formulas —if it could have anticipated them a century in advance. An imitation of an action, without obstreperous episodes or irrational gaps— this, Euripides might have felt, would be no imitation of life as *he* knew it. For the complexities of his vision, an asymmetrical form was just and proper, an objective correlative for the tormented psyche's baroque ado. Euripides (unlike Sophocles) has no *querencia;* his is a restless point of view; and if we, with our more classical habits, stay in one spot to look where he is pointing, we are likely to be left mumbling about the "riddle" of this or that play.

Modern readers may find an enlightening parallel in the work of Picasso, whom they may suspect to be the product of an analogous period: an artist who does not stare flat-footed at his subject and by whom the same face may be painted from quite different coigns of vantage. One celebrated painting shows a lady "nude, dressed, and X-rayed" all at once; it doubles the already multiple image by putting her in front of a mirror. It was with something like this simultaneous point of view that Euripides regarded his subjects; no wonder his portraits too are constructed around an ambiguous axis.

The method is used more brilliantly in the greater plays: in the *Bacchae*, for example, or *Hippolytus.* In *Andromache* the composition is twisted too violently toward propaganda; it has the stridency of caricature. The tone, it has often been observed, is not tragic at all. The events of the play may arouse pity, but they do much to counteract it by arousing the emotion that Aristotle found directly opposed: indignation. Critiques of the play bristle with such phrases as "the glaring colors of melodrama," "the air of a political pamphlet," "the whole tone unheroic," "complete absence of poetic color," "a painful experience" (for admirers of Sophoclean drama). In antiquity it was criticized as a conglomeration of comic ingredients. And yet for the theatergoer there must have been not one dull or undramatic scene in this "hard and brilliant" play.

The author of *On the Sublime* finds Euripides nearly always among those writers who use current colloquial diction. In *Andromache*, with its strongly *ad hoc* bias, colloquial usage seems even more pronounced than elsewhere; lexicographers find here boldly popular and even vulgar expressions. In reading what Norwood calls the "utterly unheroic and unpoetical, but vigorous, terse, and idiomatic" dialogue, we are far from the Olympian resonances of Aeschylus or the nobility of Sophocles, far, in fact, from what the common reader thinks of as "Greek tragedy."

The text translated here is that of Murray's Oxford edition, with his line-numbering (which corresponds to the Greek text, not to the English). I have omitted the bracketed line 7 (probably interpolated by actors), have disregarded Murray's suggested punctuation for line 1030, and have preferred Musgrave's emendation of line 1190.

CHARACTERS

Andromache, widow of Hector, allotted at the fall of Troy to Neoptolemus, son of Achilles

Slave woman

Chorus of Phthian women

Hermione, daughter of Menelaus and Helen, wife of Neoptolemus

Menelaus, king of Sparta

Young son of Andromache and Neoptolemus

Peleus, father of Achilles and grandfather of Neoptolemus

Nurse of Hermione

Orestes, son of Agamemnon and Clytemnestra, formerly betrothed to Hermione

Messenger

The Goddess Thetis

Servants, attendants

ANDROMACHE

Andromache

Thebé my city, Asia's pride, remember
The glory and the gold of that procession
When I arrived at Priam's royal home?
As Hector's wife, soon mother of Hector's son—
Andromache, in the old days oh so lucky,   5
But sunk in misery now, if anyone is.
To have seen with my own eyes Hector my husband
Dead at Achilles' hand! To have seen our son,
Hector's and mine, Astyanax, hurled headlong   10
Down from the highest tower when Troy was taken!
And I—free as I pleased in homes of leisure
Till then—was clapped in servitude, shipped to Greece
As booty for Neoptolemus, wild islander,
His tidbit from the total spoil of Troy.   15
Phthia is my home now, these fields surrounding
The city of Pharsalia. Sea-born Thetis
Lived here with Peleus once in deep seclusion,
Apart from men. The people of Thessaly
Call it the Altar of Thetis for that reason.   20
That roof you see belongs to Achilles' son,
By whose permission Peleus rules Pharsalia:
The young defers to the older while he lives.
Within that house I've given birth to a boy,
Bred to that same Achilles' son, my master.   25
A hard life even at best, but up to now
Hope led me on—the hope this little child
Might prove my strength and shelter against trouble.
Except for her—Hermione from Sparta!   30

« 75 »

Since my lord married her and snubbed a slave-wife,
I'm persecuted cruelly. She's behind it,
Charging I've made her unable to conceive
With secret drugs and dosings, made him hate her.
Charging I want this house all to myself
And mean to crowd her out of it, bed and all—   35
A bed that from the first I never wanted
And now reject for good. The gods are witness
That was a bed I never crept in gladly.
No talking, though, to her. She's out for blood.
And Menelaus her father's working with her.   40
He's in the house this moment, hot from Sparta,
Bent on this very thing. Suspecting the worst,
I've run next door here to the Altar of Thetis
And here I huddle in the hope she'll save me.
For Peleus and his sons are all devotion   45
Toward this memorial of the ocean marriage.
My one and only son, though!—alarmed for his life
I've smuggled him secretly to others' keeping.
The one who served to beget him serves for nothing
In the hour of need—no help at all to his baby.   50
He's off at Delphi making amends to Apollo
For his mad behavior when, the time before,
He clamored the god should pay for killing his father!
He hopes now to plead free of old offenses
And reconcile Apollo for the future.   55

(*Enter Slave woman.*)

Slave woman
    My lady—for I'm faithful to that title—
    I never used or thought to use another
    In your own palace when we lived in Troy.
    You always had my love—your husband too
    To the very day he died. Well, now there's news   60
    I bring in fear and trembling of our masters,
    And in sympathy for you. They've black designs,
    Menelaus and his daughter. Oh be careful!

Andromache
> Dearest of sister-slaves (for that's our story)
> To one your mistress once, though sadly fallen— 65
> They're planning what? Up to what further mischief?
> What's left to endure but death? Is that their purpose?

Slave woman
> They're aiming at your son, my poor, poor lady;
> The little boy you hid away: his death.

Andromache
> She can't have learned my darling's gone? She can't have! 70
> How could she learn? My heart stopped as you spoke.

Slave woman
> I couldn't tell you how. I heard it first
> From them. But Menelaus is out prowling.

Andromache
> My very heart stopped beating! Poor little baby,
> A pair of buzzards claw at you for carrion. 75
> And his—can I say *father?*—off at Delphi!

Slave woman
> You'd never find yourself in this predicament,
> To my mind, with him present. Now there's no one.

Andromache
> And no report that Peleus means to come?

Slave woman
> Suppose he came, what then? Feeble old man! 80

Andromache
> I've sent for him and sent for him and sent for him.

Slave woman
> Sent whom for him? No friend of yours, be sure.

Andromache
> Ah, so I see! But you—you'd take a message?

Slave woman
> What could I say, being gone from home so long?

Andromache

    Don't tell me you've no bag of tricks. A woman!   85

Slave woman

    She's wary as a watchdog, that Hermione.

Andromache

    Then you—my fine fair-weather friend—refuse?

Slave woman

    That's far from true. You've no need for reproaches.
    I'll do it. What's my life, that I should care
    What happens now? A slave's life, and a woman's.   90

Andromache

    Hurry then; hurry.

                                (Exit Slave woman.)

                   These same lamentations,
Sobbings and tears to which my days are given
I'll now storm heaven with. For nature tempers
The souls of women so they find a pleasure
In voicing their afflictions as they come.   95
I've a wide range of sorrows, not one only:
My native land destroyed and Hector dead,
The rigorous fate that shut on me like shackles
When I awoke—indignity!—to bondage.
It's vain to say that any man alive   100
Is in the true sense happy. Wait and ponder
The manner of his exit from this stage.

                               (She keens softly.)

Paris brought home no bride, no bride but folly and ruin
    To Ilium high on its hill—welcoming Helen to bed.
She was the cause, O Troy, the Greeks' quick-moving battalions   105
    Out of a thousand ships, took you with fire and sword.
She was the cause my man, wretched Andromache's Hector,
    Was draggled by Thetis' son from a chariot round about Troy.
The cause I was driven away from my quiet nook to the seashore,
    There invited to wear slavery's odious yoke.   110

What a torrent of tears on my cheek the day that I left forever
    City and roofs I knew, husband dead in the dust.
Doomed Andromache now! why longer look upon heaven?—
    Only a slave, *her* slave—one who oppresses me so
That here to the goddess' shrine I come, a suppliant clutching,   115
    Melting away, all tears, like water welling on rock.

(Enter Chorus of Phthian women.)

Chorus

STROPHE

Lady who, crouched on the ground so long by the chapel of Thetis
    Linger and will not away,
Now, though a Phthian indeed I come to you, woman of Asia,
    To see if I may   120
        Offer a balm for grievances so deep
Embittering you and Hermione too in a spite-ridden, surly,
    Hateful display:
        Over two in a post for one: 125
        The arms of Achilles' son.

ANTISTROPHE

Recognize what you've become and assent to a dismal position:
    Though only a Trojan, you sow
Seeds of unrest with your betters—with nobles from Sparta!
    Far better go
        Away from the Nereid's place of hecatomb.   130
What good to lie quivering here and sadly bedabble your features?
    Their wish is law.
        Necessity's hot on your trail.
        Why struggle to no avail?

STROPHE

Come now, hurry and leave the glorious temple of Thetis.   135
    Consider: only a slave
    Here in a foreign state,
    With no apparent friend.
    Least of all, fate—
        Girl of the gamut of woe.   140

ANTISTROPHE

A sight for compassionate eyes—my heart said—woman of Troy,
    you
Entered my masters' home.
Fear keeps me dumb,
And yet I'm all sorrow.
But what if Hermione come   145
    And find me in sympathy so?

                                        (*Enter Hermione.*)

Hermione

Wearing tiaras, notice, of pure gold,
Draped in garments brilliant and luxurious—
Neither presented to me, I hasten to add,
From the homes of Achilles or Peleus—here I am.   150
These weddings gifts are straight from my own Sparta.
Menelaus gave me these—my father you know—
With other gifts galore. I'm bound to no one
And free to speak my mind. As I do now.
You! you common slave! you soldiers' winnings!   155
You plan to usurp this house, evicting me!
Your drugs have made me unlovely to my husband;
Withered my womb and left it good for nothing.
This is the sort of thing you Asian women
Have tricky wits for. But you've met your match.   160
This sea-girl's home won't help you save your skin
For all its shrines and altars. Now you've finished!
Or if any god or mortal interfere
In your behalf—well, learn to change your tune,
Eat humble pie and grovel at my knee,   165
Sweep out the house, *my* house, your fingers sprinkling
Brook-water from the pails of beaten gold.
Just where do you think you are? Is Hector here?
Is Priam with his moneybags? You're in Greece now.
You! you were even so rotten with desire   170
You had the gall to cuddle up to the son
Of the very man who killed your husband, breeding

A butcher's children. Well, that's foreigners for you.
Father and daughter intimate, mother and son,
Sister and brother—murder clears the way   175
In family squabbles. Anything goes. No law.
Don't try those methods here. And it's not decent
Either for one man teaming up two wives.
Clean-living husbands love and honor one,
Gluing affectionate eyes only on her.   180

Chorus

There's a touch of jealousy in the female psyche.
It's inclined to be rather tart where polygamy enters.

Andromache

A sort of disease, youth is. Aggravated
When the young soul's addicted to injustice.   185
I suppose my condition of servitude should daunt me
By censoring free discussion, right as I am.
If I got the better, you'd see I suffered for it.
You high and mighty people can look daggers
Hearing from your inferiors the god's truth.   190
However, I'm one for sticking to my principles.
Speak, pretty miss: for what legitimate reason
Would I keep you from your legitimate marriage?
Troy lords it over Sparta, I suppose,
Or would with a bit of luck? I fancy I'm free?   195
Or trusting in a girl's full-breasted beauty,
A city's strength, a multitude of backers,
I'm planning to dispossess you of your home?
Or so I may have sons instead of you,
Slaves every one, like millstones dragging after me?   200
Or else so someone will exalt my boys
To the very throne itself, if you've no children?
I suppose for Hector's sake the Greeks adore me?
Or thinking I was a nobody in Troy?
It wasn't drugs that made your husband shun you;   205
The plain fact is, you're hardly fit to live with.

There's your witchcraft. It's not beauty but
Fine qualities, my girl, that keep a husband.
When something annoys you, it's always Sparta this
And Sparta that. His Skyros?—never heard of it!　　210
You flaunter among paupers! They mention your father?—
He dwarfs Achilles! No wonder your husband flushes.
A woman, even when married to a cad,
Ought to be deferential, not a squabbler.
Suppose you married a king in wintry Thrace　　215
Where the custom is one husband in rotation
Take to his bed god knows how many women.
You'd knife them all? And be in a pretty fix
Screaming, "You hussy!" at every wife in sight.
Disgraceful! Well, we women are infected　　220
With a worse disease than men, but try to conceal it.
O dearest Hector, for your sake I even
Welcomed your loves, when Cypris sent you fumbling.
I was wet nurse to your bastards many a time
Only to make your life a little easier.　　225
And for such conduct he approved and loved me.
But you!—you hardly dare to let your husband
Out in the rain. He might get wet! Your mother
Helen was fond of her man—now wasn't she, dear?
Don't try to outdo her. Sensible children　　230
Really ought to avoid the family vices.

Chorus

　　My lady, as much as you reasonably can,
　　Come to an understanding with this woman.

Hermione

　　On your high horse and picking quarrels, eh? Bragging
　　As if you had a monopoly on virtue?　　235

Andromache

　　You've none at least, one gathers from your talk.

Hermione

　　We'll never see eye to eye—or so I hope.

Andromache

Young as you are, there's smut enough on your tongue.

Hermione

And on your conscience. Doing your best against me!

Andromache

Still caterwauling your unlucky love!   240

Hermione

I'll not be gagged. Love's all in all to women.

Andromache

And should be: *virtuous* love. The other's foul.

Hermione

Here we don't live by your outlandish standards.

Andromache

Shameful is shameful everywhere, Greece or not Greece.

Hermione

We've a deep thinker here! Not long to live, though.   245

Andromache

You see this statue of Thetis, eyeing you?

Hermione

Despising your country, you mean, for Achilles' murder.

Andromache

All Helen's doing, not ours. Your mother you know.

Hermione

You strike at me where it's tenderest, more and more.

Andromache

I've said my say. You'll get no more out of me.   250

Hermione

One thing. There's still the matter that brought me here.

Andromache

I only say your mind's a twisted thing.

Hermione

Will you or won't you leave this shrine of Thetis?

Andromache
If you guarantee my life. Otherwise never.

Hermione
I'll guarantee this: your death. And before my husband comes.   255

Andromache
Until he comes, I'll not surrender. Never!

Hermione
I could light a fire, and let you take your chances—

Andromache
Light up your fire. Don't think the gods are blind, though.

Hermione
Or tools that tear the flesh—I've ways to get them.

Andromache
Make all her shrine a shambles. She'll remember.   260

Hermione
Half-savage creature, all a wild defiance!
You'd brazen out even death! I'll make you move
Out of there spryly enough and glad to go.
I've got the lure for you. Though what it is
I'll let the event itself disclose, and promptly.   265
Sit snug and cozy now. But if melted lead
Had soldered you there, I'd pry you out before
The son of Achilles comes, your one hope now.

(*Exit Hermione.*)

Andromache
My one hope now! Some god found antidotes
Against all poisonous snakes, but—wonder of wonders!—   270
Against a menace worse than fire or vipers
No vaccine yet: I mean these vicious women.
Who knows the trouble we cause the human race!

Chorus
STROPHE
That was the breeding of bitter affliction, when Hermes,
Son of Zeus, Maia's son,   275

Came to Ida, to the glade
Conducting heaven's lovely team
Of three divine fillies made
All accoutered for passionate war over who was supreme.
    These came to the farmyard   280
And sought the boyish shepherd fond of solitude—
      A hearthfire
    Where but few souls intrude.

ANTISTROPHE

These, when they reached the luxuriant vale, in a mountain pool
    Cooled by springs, shone and bathed—   285
    What a reveling of light!
And then approaching Priam's son
With glowing words born of spite
They disputed their suit. Aphrodite prevailed—witching words
    Most sweet to the young judge,   290
But deadly too, a lewd confusion to destroy
      And throw low
    All the towers of high Troy.

STROPHE

Oh but if only his mother had broken the
    Sorry creature's skull at once
      Before he
    Settled there on Ida's side—
When the marvelous laurel implored, when shrill   295
    Cassandra wild-eyed clamored "Kill
The spreading pollution of Troy, our land!"
And frenzied everywhere to needle, wheedle, warn
      Prominent men
With: "Destroy the newborn!"   300

ANTISTROPHE

    Then on the women of Troy would have fallen no
      Yoke of slavery; lady, you'd
        Have free hand,
      Mistress of a noble home;

Greece would never have shouldered the ten-years' woe
    Or seen the tall young spearmen go   305
  To the stagger of war and the ruck round Troy;
Those beds would never lie by absent love undone,
      Parents be made
    Ancient waifs with no son.

       (*Enter Menelaus with the young son of Andromache.*)

Menelaus

  I've fastened on the child you hid away
  In another house behind my daughter's back.   310
  So you thought the goddess' statue would save you
  And his receivers him? But it turned out
  You weren't as cunning as Menelaus here.
  Now either remove yourself and clear the premises
  Or the boy dies for you—a fair exchange.   315
  So think it over. The option's yours: to die
  Yourself or to see the child die for the wicked
  Wrongs you committed against my daughter and me.

Andromache

  Repute! repute! repute! how you've ballooned
  Thousands of good-for-nothings to celebrity!   320
  Men whose glory is come by honestly
  Have all my admiration. But impostors
  Deserve none: luck and humbug's all they are.
  So you're the commander-in-chief of the Greek elite
  That wrested Troy from Priam—you, you piddler!   325
  You, for the mewlings of your darling daughter
  Come snorting so importantly, up in arms
  Against a woman already down, in bondage.
  Troy's story had no role for the likes of you!
  People that seem so glorious are all show;   330
  Underneath they're like anybody else.
  Unless they have money, of course. Oh money's something!
  Well, Menelaus, suppose we thresh this out.
  Assume I lie here dead, thanks to your daughter.

The curse of bloodshed's heavy on her head.   335
A guilt that you share too, at least in the court
Of public opinion. You're involved, no question.
Or assume that I manage somehow to stay alive.
You'll kill my little child? You think the father,
His baby butchered, will stand idly by?   340
At Troy he wasn't commonly thought a coward.
He'll do the right thing now—worthy of Peleus
And of Achilles his father, as you'll find out—
He'll send your daughter packing. With what story
Do you think you'd find her another man? You'd claim   345
Her virtue was simply appalled by such a brute?
Word gets around. Who'd marry her? You'd board her
Single at home till she's a grey-haired witch?
What griefs you'd have if you kept her there, poor man!
Wouldn't you rather she'd time and again be cheated   350
In marital affairs than suffer that way?
There's no use making catastrophes of trifles.
And just because we women are prone to evil,
What's to be gained perverting man to match?
If indeed I've plied your daughter with those potions   355
And made her womb a bungler, as she charges,
I'm ready and willing to submit to trial
(Without invoking sanctuary as now)
Before your assembled kindred, in whose eyes
I'm as guilty as in yours if I made her barren.   360
There—now you know my heart. I'm worried, though,
About your famous weakness. Brawling over
A woman led you to devastate poor Troy.

Chorus
    That's quite enough from a female dealing with men.
    I'd say your righteousness had gone the limit.   365

Menelaus
    Woman, these are admittedly minor matters;
    As you say, unworthy of my regime and Greece.

But never forget: whatever one sets his heart on
Gets to be more important than taking Troy.
Being cheated out of marriage now, that matters;   370
That's why my help's enlisted for my daughter.
All other woes a woman bears are minor
But lose her husband!—might as well be dead.
It's right my son-in-law order my slaves about;
Right his be ordered about by any of us.   375
Friends—and I mean real friends—reserve nothing:
The property of one belongs to the other.
Just sitting around and waiting till men came back,
I'd be simple-minded indeed to neglect my interests.
So on your feet; get away from the goddess' shrine.   380
If you decide to die, the boy survives.
If you put your own skin first, he dies instead.
It's one of the two. No other way about it.

Andromache
Oh, here's a gloomy lottery of life,
A gloomy choosing. If I win, I lose;   385
And losing, losing—oh, I'm lost forever!
You there who make such mountains out of molehills,
Listen to reason. You're killing me—why? For whom?
What city did I betray? What child of yours kill?
Whose home set fire to? I was strong-armed into   390
A bully's bed. And it's me you kill, not him
Who caused it all? Oh, you've got everything backwards,
Punishing the effect, and not the cause.
All these troubles! O my wretched land,
What horrors I endure! Why must I bear   395
A child just to redouble throe on throe?
I who saw Hector mangled underwheel,
Who saw our Ilium blindingly afire!   400
I who came shackled to the Grecian fleet,
Haled by the hair! And, once I came to Phthia,
Knew a mock marriage with that murderous brood.

How's living sweet for me? Where should I look—
Toward yesterday's affliction or today's?   405
I had this one son left, light of my life,
And he's to be murdered by such judges now.
Murdered? Oh not to save my scraps of life.
The child has possibilities, if he lives;
And if I let him die, shame come to me.   410
So look, I'm leaving the shrine. I'm in your hands
To mangle, murder, bind, hang by the neck.
O child, the one that bore you moves toward death
And all for you. If you escape that doom
Think of your mother, what a fate she suffered!   415
And covering your father's face with kisses,
Melted in tears, crushing your arms around him,
Describe my ending. All men know their children
Mean more than life. If childless people sneer—
Well, they've less sorrow. But what lonesome luck!   420

Chorus

Her speech rouses my pity. Calamities,
Even a stranger's, call for tears in all.
Menelaus, you ought to arrange some peace between
Your daughter and this woman, instead of crushing her.

Menelaus

Now seize her, men! Lock your arms tight around her.   425
She won't take kindly what I've got to say.
Remember how I bobbled the boy's life
Before your face, to pry you off the shrine
And coax you into my clutches here to die?
You know the facts of the matter—in your case.   430
As for the boy, however—suppose we let
My daughter give the word to kill or not.
And now, get in that house. I'll teach you, slave,
To attempt assault and battery on your betters.

Andromache

Made a fool of! Duped and caught by treachery, treachery!   435

Menelaus
> Go tell the world—who cares? I'm not denying it.

Andromache
> This passes for high policy back in Sparta?

Menelaus
> Also in Troy: being struck at to strike back.

Andromache
> And there's no heaven above to punish you?

Menelaus
> Heaven I'll handle later. First things first.   440

Andromache
> You'll kill this little baby, snatched from my lap?

Menelaus
> It's out of my hands. His future's up to my daughter.

Andromache
> Then I might as well lament you now, poor darling.

Menelaus
> His prospects, it appears, are none too rosy.

Andromache
> Where's there a man that doesn't find you odious,   445
> You citizens of Sparta, devious schemers,
> Masters of falsehood, specialists in evil,
> Your minds all warped and putrid, serpentine?
> How iniquitous your prosperity in Greece!
> Name any foulness and it's yours: assassins;   450
> Your palms a tetter of itchiness; your tongues
> Off scavenging one way and your minds another.
> Damn your Spartan souls! Death's not so much
> For me as you seem to feel. I died before
> When my poor town in Phrygia was stricken,   455
> My glorious husband too, who many a time
> Whipped you, a whimpering skipper, back to your ships.
> Fine figure of a hero now, you threaten

Death to a woman. Strike! But not before
You and your daughter feel the edge of my tongue.   460
So you think you're really something now in Sparta?
Well, so was I in Troy. If I'm destroyed
You've little cause to gloat. For your time's coming.

(*Exeunt Andromache and child; Menelaus.*)

Chorus

STROPHE

Oh, I'll never approve a double love for any man,   465
   Or children born to juggled wives;
They confuse the home, bringing heavy heartaches.
   I say one man should love and honor one:
      A bride-bed
   Theirs alone till life's done.   470

ANTISTROPHE

Nor in states is it right to see a pair of princes rule:
   One tyrant's better far than two
Who indeed breed woe crowding woe and town strife.   475
   Or when two souls compose a single song,
      The muse fans
   Livid wrath before long.

STROPHE

Or when the hurricane is scudding ship and all,
   In a huddle of colloquy over the wheel, two heads   480
Are worse than one, and a panel of philosophers
   Worse than a petty but positive mind.
   Only one in command: that's the way in the home
   And the way in the state when it must find
      Measures best for mankind.   485

ANTISTROPHE

We've sad example here: the Spartan, daughter of
   Menelaus the general, is running amuck, breathes fire
Against her fellow-wife; her spite destroys the poor
   Trojan. And also her baby I fear.   490

Ungodly, unlawful, unsanctified crime!
But alas! O my queen, there's a day near
   When you'll pay and pay dear.

And indeed I see
The close-huddled pair stumble out of the house   495
Under sentence of death.
O lady so stricken, O woebegone boy
Who die on account of your parent's affairs,
Though never involved,
   Nor to blame in the eyes of the rulers!   500

(Enter Andromache and her son, hands lashed
together; Menelaus.)

Andromache

STROPHE

My hands are helpless; roped so tight,
See, there's blood where the fibers bite.
   Only the grave before me.

Son

Mother, O Mother, I'm here too
   Close to your side, to die with you.   505

Andromache

Hardly lucky this sacrifice,
Phthian counselors.

Son

          Father, do
Hurry and help if you love us.

Andromache

You'll be snuggled, my little lad,   510
Forever close to your mother's breast,
Dust with dust in the underworld—

Son

Mother, what's to become of me?
   What's for us but misery?

Menelaus

On your way to the grave! You're an enemy brood   515
From an enemy nest. You two are condemned
By a separate vote. You, woman, my voice
Has sentenced to death. And this boy of yours
By my daughter's doomed. For it's mad indeed
To let slip through your fingers inveterate foes   520
When by wiping them out
    You can free your home from its nightmare.

Andromache

ANTISTROPHE

Husband, husband, if you could stand
Here in front of us, spear in hand,
    Son of Priam, to help us.   525

Son

Dark day! Where's there a song to sing
    Likely to charm away this thing?

Andromache

Plead with him, kneel at his knees and pray,
Son, for sympathy.

Son

                    Dearest lord,   530
Don't destroy me! Oh let me go!

Andromache   .a

Only look at my tear-stained face.
How I weep, like a marble-cupped
Flowing spring in a sunless place!

Son

Poor me! Where is an opening now   535
    Out of trouble? Oh tell me how!

Menelaus

Why snivel to me? I'm hard as a rock.
You might as well make your appeal to the sea.

I've a helping hand for kith and kin,
But I'm wasting no favors, boy, on you.   540
When I think of the years of life I lost
To capture Troy and that mother of yours—!
She made your fate;
    You can pay for it six feet under.

Chorus

But look at this: old Peleus approaching   545
As hurriedly as ancient limbs can bring him.

                  (Enter Peleus, assisted by a servant.)

Peleus

I'd like to know, from you above all, head-butcher,
What's going on here? What's this? And why's the house
Become a chaos, through your lawless dealing?
Menelaus, stop. Enough felonious haste.   550
(Get me there quicker, fellow. Now's no time
For hanging back, it appears. Rejuvenation,
It's now I could do with a touch of you—now or never.)
First I'd like to put a bit of wind
In this poor woman's sails. By what right   555
Have these men strapped your hands and pushed you off,
You and the boy? Poor sheep, poor little lamb
Bound for the slaughter. All of us away!

Andromache

These, old father, are dragging me and the baby
To our grave, as you can see. What's there to tell?   560
I sent for you, though, begging desperately
Not only once but time and time again.
Surely you must have heard of the ill-feeling
His daughter roused in the house—that murderous woman!
And now from the Altar of Thetis, mother of   565
Your noble son, your own soul's adoration,
They've torn me away by force, without a trial;
Condemned me without waiting for those absent.
For knowing the baby and I were here alone

(Poor blameless innocent) they planned our murder.   570
Now I beg of you, father, crumpled here
Before your knees—for I can't get a finger free
To touch your beloved cheek in supplication—
For god's sake extricate me. Else I die—   575
Not only to my pain but your discredit.

Peleus

Loosen these knots or someone smarts for it!
Free the poor woman's cramped-together hands.

Menelaus

I've as much to say as you—in fact I've more
As far as she's concerned—and I forbid it.   580

Peleus

And by what right? You're master in my house,
Not content with lording it over Spartans?

Melenaus

She was my catch. I brought her back from Troy.

Peleus

Full rights to her passed over to my grandson.

Menelaus

Hasn't he a right to my things? I to his?   585

Peleus

To care for, not to abuse. And not to slaughter.

Menelaus

This woman, at any rate, I'll not return.

Peleus

Suppose I break your head in with this scepter?

Menelaus

Just touch me and you'll see! Only come near me!

Peleus

You call yourself a man, foul-blooded creature?   590
May I ask where you're worthy of that name?
You, who lost your own wife to a Phrygian

For leaving the house unlocked and unattended,
As if you had a decent wife indeed
Instead of the world's worst. No Spartan girl   595
Could ever live clean even if she wanted.
They're always out on the street in scanty outfits,
Making a great display of naked limbs.
In those they race and wrestle with the boys too—
Abominable's the word. It's little wonder   600
Sparta is hardly famous for chaste women.
Ask Helen—she should know. She went gallivanting
Out of her house, pooh-poohing family ties
And skipped the country with a lusty buck.
For such a slut you raised the Greek divisions   605
And led those many thousands against Troy?
You shouldn't have lifted a spear. Just sat and spat once
In her direction, when you knew her nature,
And let her stay away; why, paid to keep her there!
Not you, though. Such a thought never crossed your mind.   610
Instead, you squandered thousands of sweet souls,
Left poor old women childless in their houses,
Left grey-haired fathers weeping their strong sons.
I'm one of those bereaved ones. Bloody murderer!
I hold you accountable for Achilles' death!   615
Oh, you returned from Troy without a mark on,
All your pretty armor and regalia
Immaculate as on the day you left!
I warned my grandson, when he courted, never
To marry kin of yours, nor share his home with   620
A filthy woman's litter. They're contagious
With blotches of the mother. (Oh, be careful,
Suitors, to marry a good woman's child!)
Not to speak of your shameless conduct with your brother,
Bidding the fat-head butcher his poor girl!—   625
You, in a panic for your ladylove!
And capturing Troy—I'm on your traces, eh?—
You laid your hands on the woman and didn't kill her.

But casting sheep's eyes on her bosom, you
Unbuckled your sword and puckered up for kisses,   630
Petting that traitorous bitch, you toady of lust!
Then, coming to my grandson's in his absence
You loot his home, commit attempted murder
Atrociously on a poor mother and son
Who'll make you and your daughter rue this day,   635
Born bastard though he is. For don't forget
That poor land often outproduces rich,
And bastards get the upper hand of blue bloods.
Now get your daughter out of here. It's better
To make a poor but honest match than land a   640
No-good wealthy father-in-law. Like you.

Chorus

Out of some little thing, too free a tongue
Can make an outrageous wrangle. Really politic
Men are careful not to embroil their friends.

Menelaus

Well! hearing this, why say the old have sense,   645
Or those the Greeks regarded once as sages?
When you, the famous Peleus, so well born,
And kin to us by marriage, rave away
And blacken us, all for an alien woman.
One that you ought to whip beyond the Nile   650
And beyond the Phasis, crying on me to do so,
Seeing she comes from Asia, where so many
Of the valiant men from Hellas fell and moldered.
Your own son's blood, as well as others', on her.
For Paris, the one that killed your boy Achilles,   655
Was brother to Hector, and she's Hector's wife.
Yet you can bear to enter the same doorway,
Can bring yourself to eat at the same table;
Even let her beget her venomous offspring.
I, looking out for you as well as me,   660
Planned her removal, and you snatch her from me.

Listen (a bit of logic's not amiss):
Suppose my daughter barren, her a spawner,
You'd make her children rulers of this country,
This sacred Phthia? Men of foreign blood   665
Would order Greeks about? You think I'm foolish
Because I hold right's right? And you're the shrewd one?
Another thing: Let's just suppose your daughter
Married some citizen and got such treatment,
You'd sit back mum? I doubt it. Yet for a foreigner   670
You're yelping at your relatives by marriage?
When cheated, wife or husband feels the same.
She doesn't like it. He doesn't like it either,
Finding a frivolous woman in the house.
Yet he can mend things with his good right arm;   675
She has to count on friends' or parents' aid.
What's wrong then in my helping out my own?
You're in your doting days! My generalship,
Which you bring up, is evidence in my favor.
Poor Helen had a time of it, not choosing   680
But chosen by the gods to exalt her country.
For innocent before of arms and battles
Greece grew to manhood then. Experience, travel—
These are an education in themselves.
If coming in the presence of my wife   685
I steeled myself and spared her, I was wise.
(I always deplored, by the way, your killing your brother.)
Well, there's my speech, wise, moderate, not irascible.
If you fly off the handle, a sore throat's
The most you'll get. I find discretion pays.   690

Chorus
    Both of you stop these mad recriminations.
    It's the only thing. Before you go too far.

Peleus
    Too bad the custom here is topsy-turvy.
    When the public sets a war memorial up

Do those who really sweated get the credit? 695
Oh no! Some general wangles the prestige!—
Who, brandishing his one spear among thousands,
Did one man's work, but gets a world of praise.
Those self-important fathers of their country
Think they're above the people. Why they're nothing! 700
The citizen is infinitely wiser,
Gifted with nerve and purpose, anyway.
You were strutters at Troy, you and your brother,
Basking lazily in your high command
And sleek and fat on many another's anguish. 705
I'll show you, though, that Paris, Ida's Paris,
Was a less furious enemy than I am,
Unless you leave this house—my curse upon you!—
You and your childless daughter, that my grandson,
If he's of my blood indeed, will haul by the hair. 710
So the barren creature won't let other women
Have any children until she herself does!
Just because she's a useless reproducer
She means to keep the rest of us from families?
Get back from that woman, slaves. I'd like to see 715
If anyone interferes while I untie her.
Come, straighten up. Although I'm all atremble
I'll unloosen these tightly tangled cords.
You blackguard, look at her mutilated hands!
What did you think you were roping? Bulls? Or lions? 720
You were frightened she'd draw some weapon out and rout you?
Come over here, little boy; scoot under my arms;
Help work your mother loose. I'll bring you up
In Phthia to be a nightmare to these Spartans.
They're touted for cold steel and the hour of battle, 725
We're told. For the rest, a thoroughly inferior breed!

Chorus

Oftener than not the old are uncontrollable;
Their tempers make them difficult to deal with.

Menelaus

It's clear your inclination is toward slander.
However, I'll not resort to force in Phthia. 730
That vulgar sort of thing is quite beneath me.
For now, though—I've just remembered I'm pressed for time—
I must be leaving. There's a—there's a town
Near Sparta, in fact—it used to be quite friendly,
But now makes threatening moves. I'll take steps, 735
And with a little campaigning tranquilize it.
That matter settled to my satisfaction,
I'm coming back. With my son-in-law, man to man,
I'll have a friendly little confabulation.
If he keeps this woman in check, and from now on 740
Behaves as he should, he'll get as good from us.
If he's looking for trouble, trouble's what he'll get.
My meaning's clear: he'll reap just as he sows.
For all your blather I don't care a hoot.
Shrill as you are, you're a feeble shadow in front of me. 745
All you can ever do is talk, talk, talk.

(Exit Menelaus.)

Peleus

Go ahead, little boy, here shivering under my arms.
And you, poor woman. You've had a bad voyage, both.
But now at last you've found a quiet haven.

Andromache

O reverence, god be good to you and yours 750
For saving the baby and me in our affliction.
Be careful, though, that on some lonely road
They don't waylay us all and kidnap me,
Seeing you not so young as once, me helpless,
The boy so very little. Be on guard 755
Or, slipping free for now, we'll be seized later.

Peleus

Let's have no womanish tremors any more.
Proceed. Who dares to bother you? He'll be sorry

If he does. For under the gods (and not without
A numerous horse and foot) I'm lord of Phthia.   760
I'm still on my toes and not so old as you think.
If I so much as look hard at that fellow
He'll turn and bolt, along in years as I am.
Stout-hearted oldsters can handle the young all right.
What good are showy muscles to a coward?   765

(*Exeunt Andromache and son; Peleus.*)

Chorus

STROPHE

Best never born, if not of an affluent house,
Of fathers known to fame, with resources to match,
   Then if some appalling disaster befalls, there's   770
    Always a way for the rich.
   For those who are known to be born aristocrats,
Praise and reverence: time can never obscure the estate
   Good men bequeath: their glory (a torch on the tomb)   775
    Has no terminal date.

ANTISTROPHE

Far better not bring home a disgraceful success
Than knock awry all law with a mischievous thrust.   780
   Today's victory flatters the palate of mortals—
    Yes, but tomorrow it must
   Sour, sicken, and turn to an old deep-grown reproach.
This I always have held, to this manner of life I aspire: 785
   May no unjust sway flourish in family affairs
    Or in seat of empire.

EPODE

  White-headed Peleus, I
  Credit that tale: how at the Lapithae wedding   790
    You with the tough centaurs fought
A spectacular fight! Then on the good ship Argo rounded the
    grim cape
  Far beyond those Rolling Rocks few craft escape—

What voyage more storied than yours?   795
   Next you adventured with Heracles to Troy,
Where he, of the true stock of Zeus, hung garlands of carnage.
   Your fame fast bound to Heracles',   800
   You returned to the Greek seas.

                                     (*Enter Nurse.*)

Nurse

O my dear women, what a day we've had!
Sorrow crowding on sorrow is our portion.
The queen in the house there, poor Hermione
Left in the lurch by her father, and knowing now   805
What a heinous thing it was to attempt the murder
Of Andromache and the youngster, wants to die—
Afraid of her husband, afraid she'll be ordered out
Of the house for what she did (think of the scandal!)
Or killed for threatening lives not hers to take.   810
Her bodyguard barely managed to restrain her
From knotting the rope on her neck, then barely managed
To wrestle the sword from her hand in the nick of time.
It's clear to her now she acted badly, badly;
She's all remorse. And I—I'm quite exhausted   815
Keeping the queen from hanging herself, ladies.
Won't all of you please go into the palace now
And plead with her not to destroy herself? New faces
Have more authority than accustomed ones.

Chorus

Indeed the clamor of servants in the house   820
Substantiates your story. It's unlikely,
Poor thing, she'd keep from seizures of remorse,
Having done the things she did. Look, wild for death,
She's broken from her home and her attendants.

                                 (*Enter Hermione.*)

Hermione

               STROPHE

I'll tear out my hair by the roots; these nails   825
Will furrow my skin!

Nurse

    What are you seeking, child? Your beauty's ruin?

Hermione

ANTISTROPHE

    Torn from my curls, away, lace veil!   830
    Where the wind blows, go!

Nurse

    Cover your breast, my darling; pin your garments.

Hermione

STROPHE

    If I am bare,
    What difference here?
    Uncovered, exposed, oh terribly clear
    What I plotted against my husband.   835

Nurse

    The attempt to kill the other woman rankles?

Hermione

ANTISTROPHE

    Now I weep
    What I ventured then.
    Abominable
    In the eyes of men!

Nurse

    It's true you went too far. But he'll forgive you.   840

Hermione

    Why did you pry the
    Sword from my fingers?
    Give it back, dear friend. My final hope
    Is to strike true once. And why hide the rope?

Nurse

    What if I let you die in such distraction?   845

Hermione

    Alas my fate!
    No flames around?

No rock I can scale
To plunge in the sea? Or on forest ground?
Let the gods of the dead receive me.   850

Nurse
  Why carry on so? Divine visitations
  Come to all of us, all of us, late or soon.

Hermione
  Father, you left me derelict here
  Alone by the surf; and no ship near.   855
  It kills me; it kills me: I'll not come
  Ever again to the bridal room!
  Should I supplicate? What shrine's for me?
  Should I fall like a slave at a slave's knee?   860
  What I'd like to be
  Is a black wing leaving the Phthian shore
  Or that skiff of fir
  The earliest oar
  Drove to the end of the ocean.   865

Nurse
  Darling, I disapproved of your excesses
  When you were in the wrong against the Trojan,
  And I disapprove of this irrational panic.
  Your husband won't repudiate your marriage
  Like this, on the mere complaint of a foreigner.   870
  It wasn't you he picked up as a prize
  In Troy—a good man's your father, you had dowry
  In plenty, and your city's influential
  Far more than most. Your father's not forsaken you
  As you seem to fear; he'll see you're not rejected.   875
  Now please go in; don't make a scene in front
  Of the house. It only hurts your reputation
  If people see you here outside the palace.

Chorus
  Look! Look at this man with the foreign air
  Making so hastily in our direction!   880

(Enter Orestes.)

Orestes
Dear ladies, strangers: is this indeed the home
Of Achilles' son? the royal home and palace?

Chorus
It is. If you care to favor us with your name—?

Orestes
I'm the son of Agamemnon and Clytemnestra;
My name's Orestes. And I'm on my way   885
To the oracle at Dodona. Since I'm here
In Phthia, I thought I'd inquire about my cousin,
If she's alive and well, enjoying prosperity—
Hermione from Sparta. For although
She's living far away, she's in our thoughts.   890

Hermione
A port in a storm indeed to this sad sailor,
O Agamemnon's son! Here at your feet
I beg of you, pity the object of your care,
Doing anything but well. My arms, as urgent
As any garlands are, circle your knees.   895

Orestes
Well!
What's this? Am I seeing things, or do I really
Behold Menelaus' child, who should be queen here?

Hermione
Menelaus' child. The only one that Helen
Bore to my father there. Why shouldn't you know?

Orestes
Savior Apollo, from all this deliver us!   900
Whatever's the matter? Who's back of this, god or mortal?

Hermione
It's partly my fault. Partly too my husband's.
Partly some god's. But chaos everywhere.

Orestes

You have no children—so no trouble that way.
What else goes wrong for a woman—except her marriage? 905

Hermione

What else indeed? You've put your finger on it.

Orestes

You mean your husband loves another woman?

Hermione

He's sleeping with Hector's wife, that battle trophy.

Orestes

One man; two loves. No good ever comes of that.

Hermione

That's how it was. I acted in self-defense. 910

Orestes

Scheming against your rival, as women do?

Hermione

I wanted to see her dead. Her and her bastard!

Orestes

Did you see it through? Or did something interfere?

Hermione

Yes—Peleus, with his reverence for riffraff.

Orestes

This deed of blood—was anyone in it with you? 915

Hermione

My father. He came all the way from Sparta.

Orestes

And got the worst of it from the old man?

Hermione

Let's say he respected age. At least, he's left me.

Orestes

I see. And you've good cause to fear your husband.

Hermione

Naturally. He's within his rights to kill me.   920
What's there to say? So I beg, by the God of Kindred,
Take me out of this land, as far as possible
Or at least to my father's home. The very walls here
Seem to be howling at me: go! go! go!
All Phthia hates me. If my husband comes   925
Home from Apollo's oracle while I'm here
He'll kill me on foul charges. Or I'll be a slave
In the bastard-blooming chambers I was queen of.
"How did you fall so low?" someone may marvel.
Visits of poisonous women were my downfall.   930
They made me lose my head by talk like this:
"So you let that wretched captive, a slave in the house,
Have rights to your husband, share and share alike?
If she, in my home, meddled with my marriage
I swear by Hera that act would be her last!"   935
And I, attentive to the siren music
Of these sly, these lewd, these babbling know-it-alls,
Swelled up like a great fool. Oh why, oh why
Did I spy on my husband, having all I wanted?
Money more than enough. Control of the household.   940
The children I'd have had fully legitimate,
Hers illegitimate, half slaves to mine.
Oh, never, never—I can't say this too often—
Should a man with any sense, having taken a wife,
Let other women come and buzz around her.   945
What are they all but teachers of delinquency?
For one can make a profit by corrupting her;
Another has fallen and likes company;
Many love to make trouble—this is why
Our homes are a sink of evil. Against this   950
Double-lock your doors and bolt them too.
For not one wholesome thing has ever come
From gadabout female callers—only grief.

Chorus

    Your tongue's a little free with your own sex.
    It's understandable now. But women should   955
    Paint womanly vices in more flattering colors.

Orestes

    A piece of wise advice (whoever gave it):
    In disputations, listen to both sides.
    I was fully aware of the uproar in this house,
    The struggle between you and Hector's widow,   960
    And watched and waited to see if you thought it best
    To remain here still, or if the attempted killing
    Of the slave had terrified you into fleeing.
    I came, though you didn't appeal to me by letter,
    On the chance of talking together, as we do,   965
    Then seeing you safely away. Though mine by right,
    You're living with this man—your father's mischief!
    He gave your hand to me before invading
    Troy, and then peddled you to your present lord
    On condition he be of use in destroying the city.   970
    When the son of Achilles returned home
    (For I overlooked your father's part) I begged him
    To give this marriage up, pleading my fortunes
    And the evil genius over me—and considering
    It wouldn't be easy to marry outside the family   975
    When one had reasons for exile such as I had.
    He was highly insulting about my mother's death
    And hooted over the scarlet-clotted goblins.
    Abject, in view of that family situation,
    I was in agony, agony, but I bore it   980
    And went away halfheartedly without you.
    But now, however, since your luck is changing,
    Since you're at this impasse, without resources,
    I'll take you away and restore you to your father.
    Blood's thicker than water, and when one's in trouble   985
    Best to seek out a relative's open arms.

Hermione
About my marriage it's not for me to decide.
The whole affair is in my father's hands.
But help me away from here as quickly as possible.
My husband might come sooner than we think   990
And murder me, or old Peleus might get wind of
My escape and order the horsemen after me.

Orestes
The old man's no threat; forget him. And never fear
Achilles' son again—seeing how he scorned me.
It happens there's a death-trap set for him,   995
A noose I can't imagine a way out of,
And all of my contriving. I've said enough now—
But when it springs, the Delphian rock will know.
So he called me mother-killer? Well, I'll teach him,
If my allies at Delphi keep their word,   1000
To take in marriage women mine by right!
Black hour for him when he asked Apollo to pay
For killing his father! No last-minute repentance
Will keep the god from exacting punishment.
At Apollo's hand (my imputations helping)   1005
He'll die—I wouldn't say nicely. And taste my hate!
Let reprobates expect nothing but havoc
From heaven above: god stamps on arrogance.

                                        (*Exeunt Orestes, Hermione, Nurse.*)

Chorus
                            STROPHE

Apollo, who made Ilium's hill and its strong walls heaven-high,
Poseidon, with stallions of rain-grey flashing by   1010
        Over the moors of the sea,
    Out of fury you doomed that town—why?
    Child of your art as it was—for   1015
    Ares to wreck, who delights in the spear-hand.
        Ruined! Oh, ruined! You
    Ruined your betrayed land?

ANTISTROPHE

How many war-cars marshalled on the sand-packed riverside,
Proud horses before them! And oh how many men   1020
   Penned in inglorious strife!
  And the monarchs of Troy elate then
  With their fathers are tombed in dark earth.
  Nor on the altars of Troy any fire cries
   "Praise to the bright gods!" and no   1025
Stirring clouds of myrrh rise.

STROPHE

And Agamemnon's dead by the stroke of his wife;
She too, in the grim-faced round of a death for a death
   At her children's own hand.   1030
The god, the god shaped her name with fatal breath,
Dreaming futurity: her son from Argos marched home,
Agamemnon's in blood, and strode to the inner recess—
   Killed his own dear mother there.   1035
  O Phoebus, divine one, how credit this?

ANTISTROPHE

And mothers, scores on scores, in the markets of Greece
Made stones re-echo shrill with lament for a son,
   Wives were torn from old homes
To serve a strange husband. Not on you alone   1040
Nor on friends of yours came such distressing heartache.
But all Hellas was sick to death, and a horror of blood
   Over Troy's gay-fruited fields   1045
  Rolled like a storm pouring hell's bitter flood.

                (Enter Peleus.)

Peleus

Women of Phthia, there's something I must know.
Tell me the truth. I've heard a vague report
That Menelaus' girl has left this house
And gone off who knows where. I've come in haste   1050
To learn the facts. For when our friends are absent
The ones at home should keep an eye on things.

Chorus

You've heard correctly, Peleus. It's not fitting
For me to hide reverses that I know of.
The queen's gone from the palace. She's in flight.   1055

Peleus

Afraid of what? Out with it, the whole story.

Chorus

Afraid of her husband and her possible exile.

Peleus

On account of her cutthroat tactics toward the boy?

Chorus

Exactly. And in terror too of the slave woman.

Peleus

She left here with her father? Or someone else?   1060

Chorus

Agamemnon's son escorted her away.

Peleus

With what design in mind? Meaning to marry her?

Chorus

Meaning that and worse than that: to kill your grandson.

Peleus

By treachery? Or in fair fight, man to man?

Chorus

At Apollo's holy shrine, with a pack of Delphians.   1065

Peleus

There's danger in that, no question. Will someone go
Quick as he can to the holy hall of Delphi
And tell our good friends there what plot's afoot
Before his enemies get to Achilles' son?

(Enter Messenger.)

Messenger

Oh gloomy news!   1070

I'm under a curse to bring the news I do
To you, old father, and my master's friends.

Peleus

Ah, my clairvoyant heart's all apprehension!

Messenger

You have no grandson, Peleus—hear the worst.
Swords cut him down, so many and so sharp,   1075
In the hands of Delphians and that Mycenaean.

Chorus

What's happening to you there, old man? Don't fall.
Hold yourself up.

Peleus

                    My strength is gone. All's over.
My voice is lost. My knees are weak as water.

Messenger

If you meditate revenge for those you loved,
Don't let yourself collapse. But hear what happened.   1080

Peleus

O destiny, at the extreme verge of life
You've brought to bay a pitiful old man!
But tell me how he perished, the one son
Of my one son. I'll hear what no man should.

Messenger

When we arrived in Apollo's famous territory   1085
We spent three entire days, from dawn to dark,
Filling our eyes with all there was to see.
This aroused suspicion, apparently. For the citizens
Gathered in twos and threes, in little huddles.
The son of Agamemnon covered the town   1090
Breathing his slander into every ear:
"Notice that fellow there, who's spying on
Apollo's nooks of bullion, rich donations?
He's back again with the very thing in mind
He had before: to rifle the sanctuary."   1095

This was behind the angry rumor bruited
About the town. The directors and advisers
And other security officers, on their own,
Posted patrols among the colonnades.
But we, however, innocent of this,   1100
With sheep raised on the pastures of Parnassus
Took our places there before the altar,
Attended by our sponsors and the celebrants.
A spokesman put the question: "Now, young man,
What should we ask the god for? What's your mission?" 1105
And he: "I stand here ready to do penance
For my earlier sins against Apollo, charging
He should make payment for my father's death."
It was obvious then Orestes' word prevailed,
Branding my master a liar who really came   1110
Upon some foul design. Reaching the sanctuary
So he could pray to Apollo at the oracle,
We inspected, first, the omens of the fire.
It seems, though, that a heavily armed squad
Lay in ambush in the laurel—Clytemnestra's   1115
Son alone the brains behind this plot.
So my master faced the god and began to implore him,
When they, armed to the teeth, steel sharpened specially,
Lunged at him from behind—he wore no corselet.
But he wheeled around, not seriously hit,   1120
Whipped out his sword, snatched from beside the door
Some votive armor hanging on the pegs there,
Took a stance by the altar, every inch a warrior!
In a ringing voice he challenged the Delphians:
"Why murder one who comes as a good pilgrim?   1125
And what's the accusation I should die for?"
Not one among so many spoke a word,
Only their hands moved, pelting him with rocks.
Battered on all sides by a hail so blinding,
He heaved with rigid arm his covering shield   1130
Here, there, and everywhere, to intercept them.

No use. For many weapons came at once:
Arrows and javelins and unfastened spits,
Meat-cleavers to kill bulls clanged at his feet.
Then you'd have seen a ghastly jig, as the boy   1135
Tried to outtwist them. Men were edging around him,
Pinning him there, not giving him time to breathe,
When he suddenly rushed from the sacrificial stone,
Leaping the leap that Troy knew to its cost,
And burst upon them. They, like little pigeons   1140
Spying a falcon near, convulsed and panicked.
Many fell in the tumult, some of wounds,
Some trampled by their fellows in jammed exits,
While in the holy place unholy shrieking
Thrilled against stone. A moment of respite then—   1145
He stood spectacular in steely splendor,
Till from some deep recess a voice arose
—So weird our very flesh crept—galvanizing
The rout to a show of valor. Achilles' son
Was toppled then, a sharp sword in his ribs   1150
Thrust by a Delphian, who may claim his death
Though abetted by plenty of others. As he slumped,
Who didn't run with cold steel or a boulder
To bruise or mutilate? His handsome body
All desecrated by the berserk blows!   1155
But he lay dead almost touching the altar, so
They dragged him from the frankincense and myrrh.
We hurried the corpse away quick as we could
And now convey him here for you to weep
And wail, poor, poor old man. And so inter.   1160
All this was done by one hailed as a prophet,
Mind you, distinguisher of right and wrong—
And done to a penitent, poor Achilles' boy.
The prophet brooded, like a spiteful man,
Over wrongs done long ago. That's "wisdom" for you?   1165

(*Exit Messenger.*)

Chorus

 Oh, but look! the prince, on a litter there,
 Brought slowly home from the Delphian land!
 Poor stricken youth! And poor old man
 Who must welcome the son of Achilles home
 Not as you would if you had your wish.   1170
 But you've stumbled yourself on a desperate hour,
  One fate swamping the two of you.

   (The body of Neoptolemus is carried in by his attendants.)

Peleus

     STROPHE

 Misery! Oh what a horror to gaze upon!
 Horror to gather it into my doorway!
 This is the end for us, city of Thessaly,   1175
 Finished and done for. Never a child again,
 Never in this house.
 How I'm destroyed by calamities lashing me!
 Where's there a friend I can turn to for comforting?   1180
 Fingers I loved so! These cheeks! And these lips!
 Oh, if only your days had been numbered in Ilium
 By the Simois, that far shore.

Chorus

 He would have earned appropriate laurels then
 In death, old man, and you been far, far luckier.   1185

Peleus

     ANTISTROPHE

 Marriage, O marriage, you ruined this house of mine!
 All of this town you doomed to confusion!
 My son, my son,
 Oh, but if only that plague of your marriage, that
 Home-wrecking, child-wrecking brood of Hermione 1190
 Never had noosed you
 Tight for the death-blow, child of my child—
 Thunder and lightning ought to have blasted her!
 Nor, for the archery death to your father, should

Charges of blood have been flung at Apollo, 1195
    Divine one, by a mere man.

Chorus
STROPHE

With a cry of despair I mourn for my lost lord!
    With those rites
  Due the dead I sing this.

Peleus
  With a cry of despair I take my disconsolate turn, 1200
    An old man
  Weighted down, I weep, weep.

Chorus
  God wanted this; god brought this thing about.

Peleus
    Dearest, you've
    Left all the house a great vacancy. 1205
  You've left me alone, desolate and
  Without a son, so late in life.

Chorus
  Better you died, old man, before your children.

Peleus
    Why not wrench away my hair?
    Why not batter head and all 1210
    With savage hands? O city, see!
      Of both my boys
    This Apollo robbed me!

Chorus
ANTISTROPHE

Luckless old man who saw and felt so much!
    From now on
  What existence for you? 1215

Peleus
  Not a child, not a friend—through unabating pain
    I'll somehow
  Fumble toward my death-day.

Chorus
> In marriage the gods loved you—all for this?

Peleus
> Flown away;
> Gone for good. Oh, how far
> From those heavenly prospects they offered.   1220

Chorus
> An empty haunter of an empty house.

Peleus
> City oh no longer mine!
> Scepter, shatter on the ground!
> And you, my Nereid, girl of purple grottoes,
> How utterly
> You behold my ruin.   1225

Chorus
> Look!
> What's stirring around? What prodigy's here
> I somehow sense? Look! Look over there!
> A divinity, girls, on the shimmering air!
> And floating this way over paddock and field
> Of Phthia, nearer and nearer.   1230

>   *(Enter Thetis.)*

Thetis
> Because of our marriage, Peleus, long ago,
> I journey here from Nereus' home—your Thetis.
> First I urge you, in these present troubles,
> Not to give way to any inordinate grief.
> Even I, who never should have wept for children,   1235
> Saw the one son I bore you, dear Achilles,
> So fleet of foot—the pride of Greece!—lie dead.
> Hark and approve while I reveal my mission:
> First for the son of Achilles, cold in death here:
> Take him to Delphi; where he fell inter him;
> Let the Delphians read his stone and blush recalling   1240
> The brutal death he met at Orestes' hand.
> Next for the woman won in war, Andromache:

Fate designates, old man, her future in
Molossia, and a marriage there with Helenus.   1245
Her son goes too, the one survivor now
Of your father's line; it's destined his descendants,
King after king, at the summit of prosperity,
Will rule Molossia. Your race and mine
Is not to become extinct as now appears,   1250
Old man; no, neither is Troy's. For the gods keep
An eye on Troy, though passionate Pallas crushed it.
That you may laud our marriage to the skies,
I, a goddess born, a god my father,
Mean to release you from this human dolor   1255
And make you a divinity forever.
There in the house of Nereus, arm in arm,
Goddess with god, we'll live the future out.
And moving dry-shod over the foaming ocean
You'll see your son and mine, dearest Achilles,   1260
Lording it in his island home, on the shore
Of remote Leuké past the Hellespont.
Be off now to the sacred town of Delphi,
Escorting the corpse, and once he's under earth
Come to that grotto in the ancient reef   1265
Cuttlefish love; there take your ease until
I soar from the sea with Nereus' fifty daughters
To choir you home. What fate determines, now
Yours to effect. Great Zeus has spoken so.
And no more lamentation for the fallen.   1270
For every mother's son the gods have posted
A great assessment only death can pay.

Peleus

O royalest of companions, O my queen,
Most welcome, girl of Nereus! All these matters
You've disposed both to your glory and the children's.   1275
Farewell to sorrow at your bidding, goddess.
I'll bury this boy and hurry to Pelion's gorges

Where first I pressed your beauty in these arms.
Did I not say one ought to marry true-hearts   1280
And into honest homes, if one's for virtue?
And never yearn for dishonorable matches
Though there's a world of dowry for the having?
That way the gods are at your side forever.

(Exit Peleus.)

Chorus

Past our telling, the ways of heaven.
The gods accomplish the unforeseen.   1285
What all awaited, fails of achievement;
God arranges what none could dream.
    So in the course of our story.

THE TROJAN WOMEN[1]

Translated by Richmond Lattimore

1. This translation first appeared in *Greek Plays in Modern Translation*, edited with an Introduction by Dudley Fitts (New York: Dial Press, 1947). It is used here by kind permission of The Dial Press, Inc. Some alterations have been made, chiefly in the matter of spelling Greek names.

INTRODUCTION TO
THE TROJAN WOMEN

IN AELIAN's *Varia historica* (ii. 8), written about the beginning of the third century A.D., we find the following notice: "In [the first year of] the ninety-first Olympiad [415 B.C.] . . . Xenocles and Euripides competed against each other. Xenocles, whoever he may have been, won the first prize with *Oedipus, Lycaon, Bacchae,* and *Athamas* (a satyr-play). Euripides was second with *Alexander, Palamedes, The Trojan Women,* and *Sisyphus* (a satyr-play)."

Athens was nominally at peace when Euripides composed this set of tragedies, of which only *The Trojan Women* is extant; but Athens had only a few years earlier emerged from an indecisive ten years' war with Sparta and her allies and was in the spring of 415 weeks away from launching the great Sicilian Expedition, which touched off the next war or, more accurately, the next phase of the same war. This was to end in 404 B.C. with the capitulation of Athens.

During the earlier years of the war Euripides wrote a number of "patriotic" plays and may have believed or tried to force himself to believe in the rightness of the Periclean cause and the wickedness of the enemy. By 415 he had reason to conclude that, at least in the treatment of captives, neither side was better than the other. A group of Thebans, working with Plataean traitors, tried to seize Plataea, failed, surrendered in the belief that their lives would be spared, and were executed (Thuc. ii. 1–6). Four years later, when Plataea surrendered to the Lacedaemonians and Thebans, the entire garrison was put to death, the women were sold as slaves, and the city itself systematically destroyed (Thuc. iii. 68). About the same time the Athenians suppressed a revolt by the people of Mytilene and other cities of Lesbos. They voted to kill all grown men and enslave the women and children but then thought better of it, rescinded the order just in time, and ended by putting to death *only* rather more than a thousand men (Thuc. iii. 50). In 421 the Athenians recaptured Scione, which had revolted, put all grown men to death, and enslaved the women and children (Thuc. v. 32). In 417 the Lacedaemonians seized a small town called Hysiae and killed all free persons whom they caught (Thuc. v. 83). The neutral island city of Melos was invited, in peacetime, to join the Athenian alliance, refused, was besieged in force, and capitulated. The Athenians put all grown males to death and enslaved the women and children (Thuc. v. 116). This was in the winter of 416–415, a few months before *The Trojan Women* was presented. That same winter, the Athenians decided to conquer Sicily (Thuc. vi. 1). This expedition was, like that against Melos, unprovoked; unlike the Melian aggression, it was foolhardy, at least obviously very dangerous. It ended in disaster, and Athens never completely recovered.

The Sicilian venture had been voted and was in preparation when Euripides presented his trilogy, which, in the manner of Aeschylus, dealt with three successive episodes in the story of Troy, complemented with a burlesque of satyrs on a kindred theme. The first play is the story of Paris (Alexander), how it was foretold at his birth that he must destroy his own city, how the baby was left to die in the mountains, miraculously rescued (as such babies invariably are), and at last recognized and restored. The hero of the second story is Palamedes, the wisest and most inventive of the Achaeans at Troy, more truly wise than Odysseus, who therefore hated him and treacherously contrived his condemnation and death. While the third tragedy, our play, ends with the destruction of Troy, the prologue looks into the future, beyond the end of the action, where the conquerors are to be wrecked on the home voyage because they have abused their conquest and turned the gods against them.[1] The plot of *Sisyphus* is not known, but the Athenian poets were partial to the scandalous story that Sisyphus, a notorious liar and cheat, seduced Anticlea and was therefore the true father of Odysseus. This story is post-Homeric, as is most of the matter of the whole trilogy (Homer does not mention Palamedes, shows no knowledge of the exposure of Paris, makes Poseidon the enemy not the protector of Troy, etc.);

1. Not only is the parallel of Troy with Melos painfully close, but, with an armada about to set forth, nothing could be worse-omened than this dramatic prediction of a great fleet wrecked at sea. Aelian seems outraged that Euripides came second to Xenocles; I can hardly understand how the Athenians let him present this play at all.

it would go well with the fact that Odysseus, here seen as the unscrupulous politician, is the open villain of *Palamedes* and the villain-behind-the-scenes of *The Trojan Women*.

The effect of current events and policies on *The Trojan Women* is, I think, so obvious that it scarcely needs further elaboration, but I do not believe in the view that the play, loose as it is, is nothing but an outburst, a denunciation of aggressive war and imperialism. The general shapelessness is perhaps permitted partly because the play was one member of a trilogy; no piece which stood by itself could pass with so little dramatic action and such a nihilistic conclusion. The play-long presence of Hecuba on the stage necessitates padding, which is supplied by elaborate rhetorical debates between Hecuba and Cassandra, and Hecuba and Andromache. Out-of-character generalizations bespeak the inspirations of Euripides rather than of his dramatis personae. The trial scene of Helen is a bitter little comedy-within-tragedy, but its juridical refinements defeat themselves and turn preposterous, halting for a time the emotional force of the play. In candor, one can hardly call *The Trojan Women* a good piece of work, but it seems nevertheless to be a great tragedy.

THE TROJAN WOMEN

CHARACTERS

Poseidon

Athene

Hecuba

Talthybius

Cassandra

Andromache

Astyanax

Menelaus

Helen

Chorus of Trojan women

THE TROJAN WOMEN

SCENE: *The action takes place shortly after the capture of Troy. All Trojan men have been killed, or have fled; all women and children are captives. The scene is an open space before the city, which is visible in the background, partly demolished and smoldering. Against the walls are tents, or huts, which temporarily house the captive women. The entrance of the Chorus is made, in two separate groups which subsequently unite, from these buildings, as are those of Cassandra and Helen. The entrances of Talthybius, Andromache, and Menelaus are made from the wings. It is imaginable that the gods are made to appear high up, above the level of the other actors, as if near their own temples on the Citadel. As the play opens, Hecuba is prostrate on the ground (it is understood that she hears nothing of what the gods say).*

(*Enter Poseidon.*)

Poseidon

    I am Poseidon. I come from the Aegean depths
of the sea beneath whose waters Nereid choirs evolve
the intricate bright circle of their dancing feet.
For since that day when Phoebus Apollo and I laid down
on Trojan soil the close of these stone walls, drawn true   5
and straight, there has always been affection in my heart
unfading, for these Phrygians and for their city;
which smolders now, fallen before the Argive spears,
ruined, sacked, gutted. Such is Athene's work, and his,
the Parnassian, Epeius of Phocis, architect   10
and builder of the horse that swarmed with inward steel,
that fatal bulk which passed within the battlements,
whose fame hereafter shall be loud among men unborn,
the Wooden Horse, which hid the secret spears within.
Now the gods' groves are desolate, their thrones of power   15
blood-spattered where beside the lift of the altar steps
of Zeus Defender, Priam was cut down and died.

The ships of the Achaeans load with spoils of Troy
now, the piled gold of Phrygia. And the men of Greece
who made this expedition and took the city, stay   20
only for the favoring stern-wind now to greet their wives
and children after ten years' harvests wasted here.

The will of Argive Hera and Athene won
its way against my will. Between them they broke Troy.
So I must leave my altars and great Ilium,   25
since once a city sinks into sad desolation
the gods' state sickens also, and their worship fades.
Scamander's valley echoes to the wail of slaves,
the captive women given to their masters now,
some to Arcadia or the men of Thessaly   30
assigned, or to the lords of Athens, Theseus' strain;
while all the women of Troy yet unassigned are here
beneath the shelter of these walls, chosen to wait
the will of princes, and among them Tyndareus' child
Helen of Sparta, named—with right—a captive slave.   35

Nearby, beside the gates, for any to look upon
who has the heart, she lies face upward, Hecuba
weeping for multitudes her multitude of tears.
Polyxena, one daughter, even now was killed
in secrecy and pain beside Achilles' tomb.   40
Priam is gone, their children dead; one girl is left,
Cassandra, reeling crazed at King Apollo's stroke,
whom Agamemnon, in despite of the gods' will
and all religion, will lead by force to his secret bed.

O city, long ago a happy place, good-bye;   45
good-bye, hewn bastions. Pallas, child of Zeus, did this.
But for her hatred, you might stand strong-founded still.

                                        (Athene enters.)
Athene
    August among the gods, O vast divinity,
    closest in kinship to the father of all, may one
    who quarreled with you in the past make peace, and speak? 50

Poseidon

You may, lady Athene; for the strands of kinship
close drawn work no weak magic to enchant the mind.

Athene

I thank you for your gentleness, and bring you now
questions whose issue touches you and me, my lord.

Poseidon

Is this the annunciation of some new word spoken
by Zeus, or any other of the divinities?

Athene

No; but for Troy's sake, on whose ground we stand, I come
to win the favor of your power, and an ally.

Poseidon

You hated Troy once; did you throw your hate away
and change to pity now its walls are black with fire?

Athene

Come back to the question. Will you take counsel with me
and help me gladly in all that I would bring to pass?

Poseidon

I will indeed; but tell me what you wish to do.
Are you here for the Achaeans' or the Phrygians' sake?

Athene

For the Trojans, whom I hated this short time since,
to make the Achaeans' homecoming a thing of sorrow.

Poseidon

This is a springing change of sympathy. Why must
you hate too hard, and love too hard, your loves and hates?

Athene

Did you not know they outraged my temple, and shamed me?

Poseidon

I know that Ajax dragged Cassandra there by force.

Athene

And the Achaeans did nothing. They did not even speak.

Poseidon

Yet Ilium was taken by your strength alone.

Athene

True; therefore help me. I would do some evil to them.

Poseidon

I am ready for anything you ask. What will you do?

Athene

Make the home voyage a most unhappy coming home.   75

Poseidon

While they stay here ashore, or out on the deep sea?

Athene

When they take ship from Ilium and set sail for home
Zeus will shower down his rainstorms and the weariless beat
of hail, to make black the bright air with roaring winds.
He has promised my hand the gift of the blazing thunderbolt   80
to dash and overwhelm with fire the Achaean ships.
Yours is your own domain, the Aegaean crossing. Make
the sea thunder to the tripled wave and spinning surf,
cram thick the hollow Euboean fold with floating dead;
so after this Greeks may learn how to use with fear   85
my sacred places, and respect all gods beside.

Poseidon

This shall be done, and joyfully. It needs no long
discourse to tell you. I will shake the Aegaean Sea.
Myconos' nesses and the swine-back reefs of Delos,
the Capherean promontories, Scyros, Lemnos   90
shall take the washed up bodies of men drowned at sea.
Back to Olympus now, gather the thunderbolts
from your father's hands, then take your watcher's post, to wait
the chance, when the Achaean fleet puts out to sea.

That mortal who sacks fallen cities is a fool,   95
who gives the temples and the tombs, the hallowed places
of the dead to desolation. His own turn must come.

(The gods leave the stage. Hecuba seems to waken, and
gets slowly to her feet as she speaks.)

Hecuba

Rise, stricken head, from the dust;
lift up the throat. This is Troy, but Troy
and we, Troy's kings, are perished.   100
Stoop to the changing fortune.
Steer for the crossing and the death-god,
hold not life's prow on the course against
wave beat and accident.
Ah me,   105
what need I further for tears' occasion,
state perished, my sons, and my husband?
O massive pride that my fathers heaped
to magnificence, you meant nothing.
Must I be hushed? Were it better thus?   110
Should I cry a lament?
Unhappy, accursed,
limbs cramped, I lie
backed on earth's stiff bed.
O head, O temples   115
and sides; sweet, to shift,
let the tired spine rest
weight eased by the sides alternate,
against the strain of the tears' song
where the stricken people find music yet   120
in the song undanced of their wretchedness.

You ships' prows, that the fugitive
oars swept back to blessed Ilium
over the sea's blue water
by the placid harbors of Hellas   125
to the flute's grim beat
and the swing of the shrill boat whistles;
you made the crossing, made fast ashore
the Egyptians' skill, the sea cables,
alas, by the coasts of Troy;   130

it was you, ships, that carried the fatal bride
of Menelaus, Castor her brother's shame,
the stain on the Eurotas.
Now she has killed
the sire of the fifty sons,   135
Priam; me, unhappy Hecuba,
she drove on this reef of ruin.

Such state I keep
to sit by the tents of Agamemnon.
I am led captive   140
from my house, an old, unhappy woman,
like my city ruined and pitiful.
Come then, sad wives of the Trojans
whose spears were bronze,
their daughters, brides of disaster,
let us mourn the smoke of Ilium.   145
And I, as among winged birds
the mother, lead out
the clashing cry, the song; not that song
wherein once long ago,
when I held the scepter of Priam,   150
my feet were queens of the choir and led
the proud dance to the gods of Phrygia.

(*The First Half-chorus comes out of the shelter
at the back.*)

First Half-chorus
    Hecuba, what are these cries?
    What news now? For through the walls
    I heard your pitiful weeping.   155
    and fear shivered in the breasts
    of the Trojan women, who within
    sob out the day of their slavery.

Hecuba
    My children, the ships of the Argives
    will move today. The hand is at the oar.   160

First Half-chorus
    They will? Why? Must I take ship
    so soon from the land of my fathers?

Hecuba
    I know nothing. I look for disaster.

First Half-chorus
    Alas!
    Poor women of Troy, torn from your homes,   165
    bent to forced hard work.
    The Argives push for home.

Hecuba
    Oh,
    let her not come forth,
    not now, my child
    Cassandra, driven delirious   170
    to shame us before the Argives;
    not the mad one, to bring fresh pain to my pain.
    Ah no.
    Troy, ill-starred Troy, this is the end;
    your last sad people leave you now,   175
    still alive, and broken.

                    (*The Second Half-chorus comes out of the shelter
                                    at the back.*)

Second Half-chorus
    Ah me. Shivering, I left the tents
    of Agamemnon to listen.
    Tell us, our queen. Did the Argive council
    decree our death?
    Or are the seamen manning the ships now,   180
    oars ready for action?

Hecuba
    My child, do not fear so. Lighten your heart.
    But I go stunned with terror.

Second Half-chorus
> Has a herald come from the Danaans yet?
> Whose wretched slave shall I be ordained?   185

Hecuba
> You are near the lot now.

Second Half-chorus
> **Alas!**
> Who will lead me away? An Argive?
> To an island home? To Phthiotis?
> Unhappy, surely, and far from Troy.

Hecuba
> And I,   190
> whose wretched slave
> shall I be? Where, in my gray age,
> a faint drone,
> poor image of a corpse,
> weak shining among dead men? Shall
> I stand and keep guard at their doors,
> shall I nurse their children, I who in Troy   195
> held state as a princess?

> *(The two half-choruses now unite to form a
> single Chorus.)*

Chorus
> So pitiful, so pitiful
> your shame and your lamentation.
> No longer shall I move the shifting pace
> of the shuttle at the looms of Ida.   200
> I shall look no more on the bodies of my sons.
> No more. Shall I be a drudge besides
> or be forced to the bed of Greek masters?
> Night is a queen, but I curse her.
> Must I draw the water of Pirene,   205
> a servant at sacred springs?
> Might I only be taken to Athens, domain
> of Theseus, the bright, the blessed!

Never to the whirl of Eurotas, not Sparta   210
detested, who gave us Helen,
not look with slave's eyes on the scourge
of Troy, Menelaus.

I have heard the rumor
of the hallowed ground by Peneus,   215
bright doorstone of Olympus,
deep burdened in beauty of flower and harvest.
There would I be next after the blessed,
the sacrosanct hold of Theseus.
And they say that the land of Aetna,   220
the Fire God's keep against Punic men,
mother of Sicilian mountains, sounds
in the herald's cry for games' garlands;
and the land washed
by the streaming Ionian Sea,   225
that land watered by the loveliest
of rivers, Crathis, with the red-gold tresses
who draws from the depths of enchanted wells
blessings on a strong people.

See now, from the host of the Danaans   230
the herald, charged with new orders, takes
the speed of his way toward us.
What message? What command? Since we count as slaves
even now in the Dorian kingdom.

> (*Talthybius enters, followed by a detail of*
> *armed soldiers.*)

Talthybius
  Hecuba, incessantly my ways have led me to Troy   235
  as the messenger of all the Achaean armament.
  You know me from the old days, my lady; I am sent,
  Talthybius, with new messages for you to hear.

Hecuba
  It comes, beloved daughters of Troy; the thing I feared.

Talthybius

You are all given your masters now. Was this your dread?   240

Hecuba

Ah, yes. Is it Phthia, then? A city of Thessaly?
Tell me. The land of Cadmus?

Talthybius

All are allotted separately, each to a man.

Hecuba

Who is given to whom? Oh, is there any hope
left for the women of Troy?   245

Talthybius

I understand. Yet ask not for all, but for each apart.

Hecuba

Who was given my child? Tell me, who shall be lord
of my poor abused Cassandra?

Talthybius

King Agamemnon chose her. She was given to him.

Hecuba

Slave woman to that Lacedaemonian wife?
My unhappy child!   250

Talthybius

No. Rather to be joined with him in the dark bed of love.

Hecuba

She, Apollo's virgin, blessed in the privilege
the gold-haired god gave her, a life forever unwed?

Talthybius

Love's archery and the prophetic maiden struck him hard.   255

Hecuba

Dash down, my daughter,
the keys of your consecration,
break the god's garlands to your throat gathered.

Talthybius

Is it not high favor to be brought to a king's bed?

Hecuba
   My poor youngest, why did you take her away from me?   260

Talthybius
   You spoke now of Polyxena. Is it not so?

Hecuba
   To whose arms did the lot force her?

Talthybius
   She is given a guardianship, to keep Achilles' tomb.

Hecuba
   To watch, my child? Over a tomb?   265
   Tell me, is this their way,
   some law, friend, established among the Greeks?

Talthybius
   Speak of your child in words of blessing. She feels no pain.

Hecuba
   What did that mean? Does she live in the sunlight still?

Talthybius
   She lives her destiny, and her cares are over now.   270

Hecuba
   The wife of bronze-embattled Hector: tell me of her,
   Andromache the forlorn. What shall she suffer now?

Talthybius
   The son of Achilles chose her. She was given to him.

Hecuba
   And I, my aged strength crutched for support on staves,   275
   whom shall I serve?

Talthybius
   You shall be slave to Odysseus, lord of Ithaca.

Hecuba
   Oh no, no!
   Tear the shorn head,
   rip nails through the folded cheeks.   280

Must I?
To be given as slave to serve that vile, that slippery man,
right's enemy, brute, murderous beast,
that mouth of lies and treachery, that makes void   285
faith in things promised
and that which was beloved turns to hate. Oh, mourn,
daughters of Ilium, weep as one for me.
I am gone, doomed, undone,
O wretched, given   290
the worst lot of all.

Chorus

I know your destiny now, Queen Hecuba. But mine?
What Hellene, what Achaean is my master now?

Talthybius

Men-at-arms, do your duty. Bring Cassandra forth
without delay. Our orders are to deliver her   295
to the general at once. And afterwards we can bring
to the rest of the princes their allotted captive women.
But see! What is that burst of a torch flame inside?
What can it mean? Are the Trojan women setting fire
to their chambers, at point of being torn from their land 300
to sail for Argos? Have they set themselves aflame
in longing for death? I know it is the way of freedom
in times like these to stiffen the neck against disaster.
Open, there, open; let not the fate desired by these,
dreaded by the Achaeans, hurl their wrath on me.   305

Hecuba

You are wrong, there is no fire there. It is my Cassandra
whirled out on running feet in the passion of her frenzy.

(Cassandra, carrying a flaming torch, bursts
from the shelter.)

Cassandra

Lift up, heave up; carry the flame; I bring fire of worship,
torches to the temple.
Io, Hymen, my lord. Hymenaeus.   310

Blessed the bridegroom.
Blessed am I indeed to lie at a king's side,
blessed the bride of Argos.
Hymen, my lord, Hymenaeus.
Yours were the tears, my mother,   315
yours was the lamentation for my father fallen,
for your city so dear beloved,
but mine this marriage, my marriage,
and I shake out the torch-flare,   320
brightness, dazzle,
light for you, Hymenaeus,
Hecate, light for you,
for the bed of virginity as man's custom ordains.

Let your feet dance, rippling the air; let go the chorus,   325
as when my father's
fate went in blessedness.
O sacred circle of dance.
Lead now, Phoebos Apollo; I wear your laurel,
I tend your temple,   330
Hymen, O Hymenaeus.
Dance, Mother, dance, laugh; lead; let your feet
wind in the shifting pattern and follow mine,
keep the sweet step with me,
cry out the name Hymenaeus   335
and the bride's name in the shrill
and the blessed incantation.
O you daughters of Phrygia robed in splendor,
dance for my wedding,
for the lord fate appointed to lie beside me.   340

Chorus
    Can you not, Queen Hecuba, stop this bacchanal before
    her light feet whirl her away into the Argive camp?

Hecuba
    Fire God, in mortal marriages you lift up your torch,
    but here you throw a melancholy light, not seen

« 139 »

through my hopes that went so high in days gone past. O
    child,   345
there was a time I dreamed you would not wed like this,
not at the spear's edge, not under force of Argive arms.
Let me take the light; crazed, passionate, you cannot carry
it straight enough, poor child. Your fate is intemperate
as you are, always. There is no relief for you.   350

(*Attendants come from the shelter. Hecuba gently takes the
torch from Cassandra and gives
it to them to carry away.*)

You Trojan women, take the torch inside, and change
to songs of tears this poor girl's marriage melodies.

Cassandra

O Mother, star my hair with flowers of victory.
I know you would not have it happen thus; and yet
this is a king I marry; then be glad; escort   355
the bride. Oh, thrust her strongly on. If Loxias
is Loxias still, the Achaeans' pride, great Agamemnon
has won a wife more fatal than ever Helen was.
Since I will kill him; and avenge my brothers' blood
and my father's in the desolation of his house.   360
But I leave this in silence and sing not now the ax
to drop against my throat and other throats than mine,
the agony of the mother murdered, brought to pass
from our marriage rites, and Atreus' house made desolate.
I am ridden by God's curse still, yet I will step so far   365
out of my frenzy as to show this city's fate
is blessed beside the Achaeans'. For one woman's sake,
one act of love, these hunted Helen down and threw
thousands of lives away. Their general—clever man—
in the name of a vile woman cut his darling down,   370
gave up for a brother the sweetness of children in his house,
all to bring back that brother's wife, a woman who went
of her free will, not caught in constraint of violence.
The Achaeans came beside Scamander's banks, and died

day after day, though none sought to wrench their land from
   them   375
nor their own towering cities. Those the War God caught
never saw their sons again, nor were they laid to rest
decently in winding sheets by their wives' hands, but lie
buried in alien ground; while all went wrong at home
as the widows perished, and barren couples raised and nursed   380
the children of others, no survivor left to tend
the tombs, and what is left there, with blood sacrificed.
For such success as this congratulate the Greeks.
No, but the shame is better left in silence, for fear
my singing voice become the voice of wretchedness.   385
The Trojans have that glory which is loveliest:
they died for their own country. So the bodies of all
who took the spears were carried home in loving hands,
brought, in the land of their fathers, to the embrace of earth
and buried becomingly as the rite fell due. The rest,   390
those Phrygians who escaped death in battle, day by day
came home to happiness the Achaeans could not know;
their wives, their children. Then was Hector's fate so sad?
You think so. Listen to the truth. He is dead and gone
surely, but with reputation, as a valiant man.   395
How could this be, except for the Achaeans' coming?
Had they held back, none might have known how great he
   was.
The bride of Paris was the daughter of Zeus. Had he
not married her, fame in our house would sleep in silence still.
Though surely the wise man will forever shrink from war,   400
yet if war come, the hero's death will lay a wreath
not lustreless on the city. The coward alone brings shame.
Let no more tears fall, Mother, for our land, nor for
this marriage I make; it is by marriage that I bring
to destruction those whom you and I have hated most.   405

Chorus
    You smile on your disasters. Can it be that you
    some day will illuminate the darkness of this song?

Talthybius
   Were it not Apollo who has driven wild your wits
   I would make you sorry for sending the princes of our host
   on their way home in augury of foul speech like this.   410
   Now pride of majesty and wisdom's outward show
   have fallen to stature less than what was nothing worth
   since he, almighty prince of the assembled Hellenes,
   Atreus' son beloved, has stooped—by his own will—
   to find his love in a crazed girl. I, a plain man,   415
   would not marry this woman or keep her as my slave.
   You then, with your wits unhinged by idiocy,
   your scolding of Argos and your Trojans glorified
   I throw to the winds to scatter them. Come now with me
   to the ships, a bride—and such a bride—for Agamemnon.   420

   Hecuba, when Laertes' son calls you, be sure
   you follow; if what all say who came to Ilium
   is true, at the worst you will be a good woman's slave.

Cassandra
   That servant is a vile thing. Oh, how can heralds keep
   their name of honor? Lackeys for despots be they, or   425
   lackeys to the people, all men must despise them still.
   You tell me that my mother must be slave in the house
   of Odysseus? Where are all Apollo's promises
   uttered to me, to my own ears, that Hecuba
   should die in Troy? Odysseus I will curse no more,   430
   poor wretch, who little dreams of what he must go through
   when he will think Troy's pain and mine were golden grace
   beside his own luck. Ten years he spent here, and ten
   more years will follow before he at last comes home, forlorn
   after the terror of the rock and the thin strait,   435
   Charybdis; and the mountain striding Cyclops, who eats
   men's flesh; the Ligyan witch who changes men to swine,
   Circe; the wreck of all his ships on the salt sea,
   the lotus passion, the sacred oxen of the Sun

slaughtered, and dead flesh moaning into speech, to make   440
Odysseus listening shiver. Cut the story short:
he will go down to the water of death, and return alive
to reach home and the thousand sorrows waiting there.

Why must I transfix each of Odysseus' labors one by one?
Lead the way quick to the house of death where I shall
    take my mate.   445
Lord of all the sons of Danaus, haughty in your mind of pride,
not by day, but evil in the evil night you shall find your grave
when I lie corpse-cold and naked next my husband's sepulcher,
piled in the ditch for animals to rip and feed on, beaten by
streaming storms of winter, I who wore Apollo's sacraments.   450
Garlands of the god I loved so well, the spirit's dress of pride,
leave me, as I leave those festivals where once I was so gay.
See, I tear your adornments from my skin not yet defiled by
    touch,
throw them to the running winds to scatter, O lord of prophecy,
Where is this general's ship, then? Lead me where I must set my
    feet on board.   455
Wait the wind of favor in the sails; yet when the ship goes out
from this shore, she carries one of the three Furies in my shape.
Land of my ancestors, good-bye; O Mother, weep no more for
    me.
You beneath the ground, my brothers, Priam, father of us all,
I will be with you soon and come triumphant to the dead below,   460
leaving behind me, wrecked, the house of Atreus, which de-
    stroyed our house.

        (*Cassandra is taken away by Talthybius and his soldiers.*
                    Hecuba collapses.)

Chorus
    Handmaids of aged Hecuba, can you not see
    how your mistress, powerless to cry out, lies prone? Oh, take
    her hand and help her to her feet, you wretched maids.
    Will you let an aged helpless woman lie so long?   465

Hecuba

No. Let me lie where I have fallen. Kind acts, my maids,
must be unkind, unwanted. All that I endure
and have endured and shall, deserves to strike me down.
O gods! What wretched things to call on—gods!—for help
although the decorous action is to invoke their aid   470
when all our hands lay hold on is unhappiness.
No. It is my pleasure first to tell good fortune's tale,
to cast its count more sadly against disasters now.
I was a princess, who was once a prince's bride,
mother by him of sons pre-eminent, beyond   475
the mere numbers of them, lords of the Phrygian domain,
such sons for pride to point to as no woman of Troy,
no Hellene, none in the outlander's wide world might match.
And then I saw them fall before the spears of Greece,
and cut this hair for them, and laid it on their graves.   480
I mourned their father, Priam. None told me the tale
of his death. I saw it, with these eyes. I stood to watch
his throat cut, next the altar of the protecting god.
I saw my city taken. And the girls I nursed,
choice flowers to wear the pride of any husband's eyes,   485
matured to be dragged by hands of strangers from my arms.
There is no hope left that they will ever see me more,
no hope that I shall ever look on them again.
There is one more stone to key this arch of wretchedness:
I must be carried away to Hellas now, an old   490
slave woman, where all those tasks that wrack old age shall be
given me by my masters. I must work the bolt
that bars their doorway, I whose son was Hector once;
or bake their bread; lay down these withered limbs to sleep
on the bare ground, whose bed was royal once; abuse   495
this skin once delicate the slattern's way, exposed
through robes whose rags will mock my luxury of long since.
Unhappy, O unhappy. And all this came to pass
and shall be, for the way one woman chose a man.
Cassandra, O Daughter, whose excitements were the god's,   500

you have paid for your consecration now; at what a price!
And you, my poor Polyxena, where are you now?
Not here, nor any boy or girl of mine, who were
so many once, is near me in my unhappiness.
And you would lift me from the ground? What hope? What use?   505
Guide these feet long ago so delicate in Troy,
a slave's feet now, to the straw sacks laid on the ground
and the piled stones; let me lay down my head and die
in an exhaustion of tears. Of all who walk in bliss
call not one happy yet, until the man is dead.   510

*(Hecuba, after being led to the back of the stage, flings herself
to the ground once more.)*

Chorus
   Voice of singing, stay
   with me now, for Ilium's sake;
   take up the burden of tears,
   the song of sorrow;
   the dirge for Troy's death   515
   must be chanted;
   the tale of my captivity
   by the wheeled stride of the four-foot beast of the Argives,
   the horse they left in the gates,
   thin gold at its brows,   520
   inward, the spears' high thunder.
   Our people thronging
   the rock of Troy let go the great cry:
   "The war is over! Go down,
   bring back the idol's enchanted wood   525
   to the Maiden of Ilium, Zeus' daughter."
   Who stayed then? Not one girl, not one
   old man, in their houses,
   but singing for happiness
   let the lurking death in.   530

   And the generation of Troy
   swept solid to the gates

to give the goddess
her pleasure: the colt immortal, unbroken,
the nest of Argive spears,
death for the children of Dardanus   535
sealed in the sleek hill pine chamber.
In the sling of the flax twist shipwise
they berthed the black hull
in the house of Pallas Athene   540
stone paved, washed now in the blood of our people.
Strong, gay work
deep into black night
to the stroke of the Libyan lute
and all Troy singing, and girls'   545
light feet pulsing the air
in the kind dance measures;
indoors, lights everywhere,
torchflares on black
to forbid sleep's onset.   550

I was there also: in the great room
I danced the maiden of the mountains,
Artemis, Zeus' daughter.
When the cry went up, sudden,   555
bloodshot, up and down the city, to stun
the keep of the citadel. Children
reached shivering hands to clutch
at the mother's dress.
War stalked from his hiding place.   560
Pallas did this.
Beside their altars the Trojans
died in their blood. Desolate now,
men murdered, our sleeping rooms gave up
their brides' beauty   565
to breed sons for Greek men,
sorrow for our own country.

*(A wagon comes on the stage. It is heaped with a number of
spoils of war, in the midst of which sits Andromache
holding Astyanax. While the chorus continues
speaking, Hecuba rises once more.)*

Hecuba look, I see her, rapt
to the alien wagon, Andromache,
close to whose beating breast clings   570
the boy Astyanax, Hector's sweet child.
O carried away—to what land?—unhappy woman,
on the wagon floor, with the brazen arms
of Hector, of Troy
captive and heaped beside you,
torn now from Troy, for Achilles' son   575
to hang in the shrines of Phthia.

Andromache
   I am in the hands of Greek masters.

Hecuba
   Alas!

Andromache
     Must the incantation

Hecuba
   (ah me!)

Andromache
       of my own grief win tears from you?

Hecuba
   It must—O Zeus!

Andromache
         My own distress?   580

Hecuba
   O my children

Andromache
       once. No longer.

Hecuba
   Lost, lost, Troy our dominion

Andromache
  unhappy

Hecuba
      and my lordly children.

Andromache
  Gone, alas!

Hecuba
        They were mine.

Andromache
  Sorrows only.

Hecuba
          Sad destiny   585

Andromache
  of our city

Hecuba
        a wreck, and burning.

Andromache
  Come back, O my husband.

Hecuba
  Poor child, you invoke
  a dead man; my son once

Andromache
  my defender.   590

Hecuba
  And you, whose death shamed the Achaeans,

Andromache
  lord of us all once,
  O patriarch, Priam,

Hecuba
  take me to my death now.

Andromache
  Longing for death drives deep;

Hecuba

O sorrowful, such is our fortune;   595

Andromache
  lost our city

Hecuba

and our pain lies deep under pain piled over.

Andromache
  We are the hated of God, since once your youngest escaping
  death, brought down Troy's towers in the arms of a worthless
    woman,
  piling at the feet of Pallas the bleeding bodies of our young men
  sprawled, kites' food, while Troy takes up the yoke of captivity.   600

Hecuba
  O my city, my city forlorn

Andromache
                    abandoned, I weep this

Hecuba
  miserable last hour

Andromache
                    of the house where I bore my children.

Hecuba
  O my sons, this city and your mother are desolate of you.
  Sound of lamentation and sorrow,
  tears on tears shed. Home, farewell, since the dead have forgotten   605
  all sorrows, and weep no longer.

Chorus
  They who are sad find somehow sweetness in tears, the song
  of lamentation and the melancholy Muse.

Andromache
  Hecuba, mother of the man whose spear was death   610
  to the Argives, Hector: do you see what they have done to us?

Hecuba
  I see the work of gods who pile tower-high the pride
  of those who were nothing, and dash present grandeur down.

Andromache
> We are carried away, sad spoils, my boy and I; our life
> transformed, as the aristocrat becomes the serf.   615

Hecuba
> Such is the terror of necessity. I lost
> Cassandra, roughly torn from my arms before you came.

Andromache
> Another Ajax to haunt your daughter? Some such thing
> it must be. Yet you have lost still more than you yet know.

Hecuba
> There is no numbering my losses. Infinitely   620
> misfortune comes to outrace misfortune known before.

Andromache
> Polyxena is dead. They cut your daughter's throat
> to pleasure dead Achilles' corpse, above his grave.

Hecuba
> O wretched. This was what Talthybius meant, that speech
> cryptic, incomprehensible, yet now so clear.   625

Andromache
> I saw her die, and left this wagon seat to lay
> a robe upon her body and sing the threnody.

Hecuba
> Poor child, poor wretched, wretched darling, sacrificed,
> but without pity, and in pain, to a dead man.

Andromache
> She is dead, and this was death indeed; and yet to die   630
> as she did was better than to live as I live now.

Hecuba
> Child, no. No life, no light is any kind of death,
> since death is nothing, and in life the hopes live still.

Andromache
> O Mother, our mother, hear me while I reason through
> this matter fairly—might it even hush your grief?   635

Death, I am sure, is like never being born, but death
is better thus by far than to live a life of pain,
since the dead with no perception of evil feel no grief,
while he who was happy once, and then unfortunate,
finds his heart driven far from the old lost happiness.   640
She died; it is as if she never saw the light
of day, for she knows nothing now of what she suffered.
But I, who aimed the arrows of ambition high
at honor, and made them good, see now how far I fall,
I, who in Hector's house worked out all custom that brings   645
discretion's name to women. Blame them or blame them not,
there is one act that swings the scandalous speech their way
beyond all else: to leave the house and walk abroad.
I longed to do it, but put the longing aside, and stayed
always within the inclosure of my own house and court.   650
The witty speech some women cultivate I would
not practice, but kept my honest inward thought, and made
my mind my only and sufficient teacher. I gave
my lord's presence the tribute of hushed lips, and eyes
quietly downcast. I knew when my will must have its way   655
over his, knew also how to give way to him in turn.
Men learned of this; I was talked of in the Achaean camp,
and reputation has destroyed me now. At the choice
of women, Achilles' son picked me from the rest, to be
his wife: a lordly house, yet I shall be a slave.   660
If I dash back the beloved memory of Hector
and open wide my heart to my new lord, I shall be
a traitor to the dead love, and know it; if I cling
faithful to the past, I win my master's hatred. Yet
they say one night of love suffices to dissolve   665
a woman's aversion to share the bed of any man.
I hate and loathe that woman who casts away the once
beloved, and takes another in her arms of love.
Even the young mare torn from her running mate and teamed
with another will not easily wear the yoke. And yet   670
this is a brute and speechless beast of burden, not

like us intelligent, lower far in nature's scale.
Dear Hector, when I had you I had a husband, great
in understanding, rank, wealth, courage: all my wish.
I was a virgin when you took me from the house   675
of my father; I gave you all my maiden love, my first,
and now you are dead, and I must cross the sea, to serve,
prisoner of war, the slave's yoke on my neck, in Greece.
No, Hecuba; can you not see my fate is worse
than hers you grieve, Polyxena's? That one thing left   680
always while life lasts, hope, is not for me. I keep
no secret deception in my heart—sweet though it be
to dream—that I shall ever be happy any more.

Chorus

You stand where I do in misfortune, and while you mourn
your own life, tell me what I, too, am suffering.   685

Hecuba

I have never been inside the hull of a ship, but know
what I know only by hearsay and from painted scenes,
yet think that seamen, while the gale blows moderately,
take pains to spare unnecessary work, and send
one man to the steering oar, another aloft, and crews   690
to pump the bilge from the hold. But when the tempest comes,
and seas wash over the decks they lose their nerve, and let
her go by the run at the waves' will, leaving all to chance.
So I, in this succession of disasters, swamped,
battered by this storm immortally inspired, have lost   695
my lips' control and let them go, say anything
they will. Yet still, beloved child, you must forget
what happened with Hector. Tears will never save you now.
Give your obedience to the new master; let your ways
entice his heart to make him love you. If you do   700
it will be better for all who are close to you. This boy,
my own son's child, might grow to manhood and bring back—
he alone could do it—something of our city's strength.

On some far day the children of your children might
come home, and build. There still may be another Troy.   705

But *we* say this, and others will speak also. See,
here is some runner of the Achaeans come again.
Who is he? What news? What counsel have they taken now?

(*Talthybius enters again with his escort.*)

Talthybius
O wife of Hector, once the bravest man in Troy,
do not hate me. This is the will of the Danaans and   710
the kings. I wish I did not have to give this message.

Andromache
What can this mean, this hint of hateful things to come?

Talthybius
The council has decreed for your son—how can I say this?

Andromache
That he shall serve some other master than I serve?

Talthybius
No man of Achaea shall ever make this boy his slave.   715

Andromache
Must he be left behind in Phrygia, all alone?

Talthybius
Worse; horrible. There is no easy way to tell it.

Andromache
I thank your courtesy—unless your news be really good.

Talthybius
They will kill your son. It is monstrous. Now you know the truth.

Andromache
Oh, this is worse than anything I heard before.   720

Talthybius
Odysseus. He urged it before the Greeks, and got his way.

Andromache
This is too much grief, and more than anyone could bear.

Talthybius
He said a hero's son could not be allowed to live.

Andromache
Even thus may his own sons some day find no mercy.

Talthybius
He must be hurled from the battlements of Troy.

>   (*He goes toward Andromache, who clings fast
>   to her child, as if to resist.*)

                                    No, wait!   725
Let it happen this way. It will be wiser in the end.
Do not fight it. Take your grief as you were born to take it,
give up the struggle where your strength is feebleness
with no force anywhere to help. Listen to me!
Your city is gone, your husband. You are in our power.   730
How can one woman hope to struggle against the arms
of Greece? Think, then. Give up the passionate contest.

                                              This
will bring no shame. No man can laugh at your submission.
And please—I request you—hurl no curse at the Achaeans
for fear the army, savage over some reckless word,   735
forbid the child his burial and the dirge of honor.
Be brave, be silent; out of such patience you can hope
the child you leave behind will not lie unburied here,
and that to you the Achaeans will be less unkind.

Andromache
O darling child I loved too well for happiness,   740
your enemies will kill you and leave your mother forlorn.
Your own father's nobility, where others found
protection, means your murder now. The memory
of his valor comes ill-timed for you. O bridal bed,
O marriage rites that brought me home to Hector's house   745
a bride, you were unhappy in the end. I lived
never thinking the baby I had was born for butchery
by Greeks, but for lordship over all Asia's pride of earth.

Poor child, are you crying too? Do you know what they
will do to you? Your fingers clutch my dress. What use,   750
to nestle like a young bird under the mother's wing?
Hector cannot come back, not burst from underground
to save you, that spear of glory caught in the quick hand,
nor Hector's kin, nor any strength of Phrygian arms.
Yours the sick leap head downward from the height, the fall 755
where none have pity, and the spirit smashed out in death.
O last and loveliest embrace of all, O child's
sweet fragrant body. Vanity in the end. I nursed
for nothing the swaddled baby at this mother's breast;
in vain the wrack of the labor pains and the long sickness. 760
Now once again, and never after this, come close
to your mother, lean against my breast and wind your arms
around my neck, and put your lips against my lips.

(She kisses Astyanax and relinquishes him.)

Greeks! Your Greek cleverness is simple barbarity.
Why kill this child, who never did you any harm?   765
O flowering of the house of Tyndareus! Not his,
not God's daughter, never that, but child of many fathers
I say; the daughter of Vindictiveness, of Hate,
of Blood, Death; of all wickedness that swarms on earth.
I cry it aloud: Zeus never was your father, but you   770
were born a pestilence to all Greeks and the world beside.
Accursed; who from those lovely and accursed eyes
brought down to shame and ruin the bright plains of Troy.
Oh, seize him, take him, dash him to death if it must be done;
feed on his flesh if it is your will. These are the gods   775
who damn us to this death, and I have no strength to save
my boy from execution. Cover this wretched face
and throw me into the ship and that sweet bridal bed
I walk to now across the death of my own child.

(Talthybius gently lifts the child out of the wagon, which
leaves the stage, carrying Andromache away.)

Chorus

    Unhappy Troy! For the sweetness in one woman's arms'   780
    embrace, unspeakable, you lost these thousands slain.

Talthybius

    Come, boy, taken from the embrace beloved
    of your mourning mother. Climb the high circle
    of the walls your fathers built. There
    end life. This was the order.   785
    Take him.

               (*He hands Astyanax to the guards, who lead him out.*)
          I am not the man
    to do this. Some other
    without pity, not as I ashamed,
    should be herald of messages like this.

                                    (*He goes out.*)

Hecuba

    O child of my own unhappy child,   790
    shall your life be torn from your mother
    and from me? Wicked. Can I help,
    dear child, not only suffer? What help?
    Tear face, beat bosom. This is all
    my power now. O city,   795
    O child, what have we left to suffer?
    Are we not hurled
    down the whole length of disaster?

Chorus

    Telamon, O king in the land where the bees swarm,
    Salamis the surf-pounded isle where you founded your city   800
    to front that hallowed coast where Athene broke
    forth the primeval pale branch of olive,
    wreath of the bright air and a glory on Athens the shining:
    O Telamon, you came in your pride of arms
    with Alcmena's archer   805
    to Ilium, our city, to sack and destroy it
    on that age-old venture.

This was the first flower of Hellenic strength Heracles brought
   in anger
for the horses promised; and by Simois' calm waters   810
checked the surf-wandering oars and made fast the ships' stern
   cables.
From which vessels came out the deadly bow hand,
death to Laomedon, as the scarlet wind of the flames swept over
masonry straight-hewn by the hands of Apollo.   815
This was a desolation of Troy
twice taken; twice in the welter of blood the walls Dardanian
went down before the red spear.

In vain, then, Laomedon's child,   820
you walk in delicate pride
by the golden pitchers
in loveliest servitude
to fill Zeus' wine cups;
while Troy your mother is given to the flame to eat,   825
and the lonely beaches
mourn, as sad birds sing
for the young lost,   830
for the sword hand and the children
and the aged women.
Gone now the shining pools where you bathed,
the fields where you ran
all desolate. And you,
Ganymede, go in grace by the thrones of God   835
with your young, calm smile even now
as Priam's kingdom
falls to the Greek spear.   840

O Love, Love, it was you
in the high halls of Dardanus,
the sky-daughters of melody beside you,
who piled the huge strength of Troy
in towers, the gods' own hands   845
concerned. I speak no more

against Zeus' name.
But the light men love, who shines
through the pale wings of morning,
balestar on this earth now,   850
watched the collapse of tall towers:
Dawn. Her lord was of this land;
she bore his children,
Tithonus, caught away by the golden car
and the starry horses,   855
who made our hopes so high.
For the gods loved Troy once.
Now they have forgotten.

*(Menelaus comes on the stage, attended by a detail of
armed soldiers.)*

Menelaus

O splendor of sunburst breaking forth this day, whereon   860
I lay my hands once more on Helen, my wife. And yet
it is not, so much as men think, for the woman's sake
I came to Troy, but against that guest proved treacherous,   865
who like a robber carried the woman from my house.
Since the gods have seen to it that *he* paid the penalty,
fallen before the Hellenic spear, his kingdom wrecked,
I come for *her* now, the wife once my own, whose name
I can no longer speak with any happiness,   870
to take her away. In this house of captivity
she is numbered among the other women of Troy, a slave.
And those men whose work with the spear has won her back
gave her to me, to kill, or not to kill, but lead
away to the land of Argos, if such be my pleasure.   875
And such it is; the death of Helen in Troy I will let
pass, have the oars take her by sea ways back to Greek
soil, and there give her over to execution;
blood penalty for friends who are dead in Ilium here.
Go to the house, my followers, and take her out;   880
no, drag her out; lay hands upon that hair so stained

with men's destruction. When the winds blow fair astern
we will take ship again and bring her back to Hellas.

Hecuba

O power, who mount the world, wheel where the world rides,
O mystery of man's knowledge, whosoever you be,   885
Zeus named, nature's necessity or mortal mind,
I call upon you; for you walk the path none hears
yet bring all human action back to right at last.

Menelaus

What can this mean? How strange a way to call on gods.

Hecuba

Kill your wife, Menelaus, and I will bless your name.   890
But keep your eyes away from her. Desire will win.
She looks enchantment, and where she looks homes are set fire;
she captures cities as she captures the eyes of men.
We have had experience, you and I. We know the truth.

> (*Men at arms bring Helen roughly out of the shelter.*
> *She makes no resistance.*)

Helen

Menelaus, your first acts are argument of terror   895
to come. Your lackeys put their hands on me. I am dragged
out of my chambers by brute force. I know you hate
me; I am almost sure. And still there is one question
I would ask you, if I may. What have the Greeks decided
to do with me? Or shall I be allowed to live?   900

Menelaus

You are not strictly condemned, but all the army gave
you into my hands, to kill you for the wrong you did.

Helen

Is it permitted that I argue this, and prove
that my death, if I am put to death, will be unjust?

Menelaus

I did not come to talk with you. I came to kill.   905

« 159 »

Hecuba

No, Menelaus, listen to her. She should not die
unheard. But give me leave to take the opposite case;
the prosecution. There are things that happened in Troy
which you know nothing of, and the long-drawn argument
will mean her death. She never can escape us now.   910

Menelaus

This is a gift of leisure. If she wishes to speak
she may. But it is for your sake, understand, that I give
this privilege I never would have given to her.

Helen

Perhaps it will make no difference if I speak well
or badly, and your hate will not let you answer me.   915
All I can do is to foresee the arguments
you will use in accusation of me, and set against
the force of your charges, charges of my own.
                                                        First, then!
She mothered the beginning of all this wickedness.
For Paris was her child. And next to her the old king,   920
who would not destroy the infant Alexander, that dream
of the firebrand's agony, has ruined Troy, and me.
This is not all; listen to the rest I have to say.
Alexander was the judge of the goddess trinity.
Pallas Athene would have given him power, to lead   925
the Phrygian arms on Hellas and make it desolate.
All Asia was Hera's promise, and the uttermost zones
of Europe for his lordship, if her way prevailed.
But Aphrodite, picturing my loveliness,
promised it to him, if he would say her beauty surpassed   930
all others. Think what this means, and all the consequence.
Cypris prevailed, and I was won in marriage: all
for Greek advantage. Asia is not your lord; you serve
no tyrant now, nor take the spear in his defense.
Yet Hellas' fortune was my own misfortune. I,   935

sold once for my body's beauty stand accused, who should
for what has been done wear garlands on my head.

I know.

You will say all this is nothing to the immediate charge:
I did run away; I did go secretly from your house.
But when he came to me—call him any name you will: 940
Paris? or Alexander? or the spirit of blood
to haunt this woman?—he came with a goddess at his side;
no weak one. And you—it was criminal—took ship for Crete
and left me there in Sparta in the house, alone.

You see?

I wonder—and I ask this of myself, not you—   945
why *did* I do it? What made me run away from home
with the stranger, and betray my country and my hearth?
Challenge the goddess then, show your greater strength than
    Zeus'
who has the other gods in his power, and still is slave
to Aphrodite alone. Shall I not be forgiven?   950
Still you might have some show of argument against me.
When Paris was gone to the deep places of death, below
ground, and the immortal practice on my love was gone,
I should have come back to the Argive ships, left Troy.
I did try to do it, and I have witnesses,   955
the towers' gatekeepers and the sentinels on the wall,
who caught me again and again as I let down the rope
from the battlements and tried to slip away to the ground.
For Deiphobus, my second husband: he took me away
by force and kept me his wife against the Phrygians' will.   960

O my husband, can you kill me now and think you kill
in righteousness? I was the bride of force. Before,
I brought their houses to the sorrow of slavery
instead of conquest. Would you be stronger than the gods?
Try, then. But even such ambition is absurd.   965

Chorus

O Queen of Troy, stand by your children and your country!
Break down the beguilement of this woman, since she speaks
well, and has done wickedly. This is dangerous.

Hecuba

First, to defend the honor of the gods, and show
that the woman is a scandalous liar. I will not   970
believe it! Hera and the virgin Pallas Athene
could never be so silly and empty-headed
that Hera would sell Argos to the barbarians,
or Pallas let Athenians be the slaves of Troy.
They went to Ida in girlish emulation, vain   975
of their own loveliness? Why? Tell me the reason Hera
should fall so much in love with the idea of beauty.
To win some other lord more powerful than Zeus?
Or has Athene marked some god to be her mate,
she, whose virginity is a privilege won from Zeus,   980
who abjures marriage? Do not trick out your own sins
by calling the gods stupid. No wise man will believe you.
You claim, and I must smile to hear it, that Aphrodite
came at my son's side to the house of Menelaus;
who could have caught up you and your city of Amyclae   985
and set you in Ilium, moving not from the quiet of heaven.
Nonsense. My son was handsome beyond all other men.
You looked at him, and sense went Cyprian at the sight,
since Aphrodite is nothing but the human lust,
named rightly, since the word of lust begins the god's name.   990
You saw him in the barbaric splendor of his robes,
gorgeous with gold. It made your senses itch. You thought,
being queen only in Argos, in little luxury,
that once you got rid of Sparta for the Phrygian city
where gold streamed everywhere, you could let extravagance   995
run wild. No longer were Menelaus and his house
sufficient to your spoiled luxurious appetites.

So much for that. You say my son took you away
by force. What Spartan heard you cry for help? You did
cry out? Or did you? Castor, your brother, was there, a young   1000
man, and his twin not yet caught up among the stars.
Then when you had reached Troy, and the Argives at your heels
came, and the agony of the murderous spears began,
when the reports came in that Menelaus' side
was winning, you would praise him, simply to make my son   1005
unhappy at the strength of his love's challenger,
forgetting your husband when the luck went back to Troy.
You worked hard: not to make yourself a better woman,
but to make sure always to be on the winning side.
You claim you tried to slip away with ropes let down   1010
from the ramparts, and this proves you stayed against your will?
Perhaps. But when were you ever caught in the strangling noose,
caught sharpening a dagger? Which any noble wife
would do, desperate with longing for her lord's return.
Yet over and over again I gave you good advice: 1015
"Make your escape, my daughter; there are other girls
for my sons to marry. I will help you get away
to the ships of the Achaeans. Let the Greeks, and us,
stop fighting." So I argued, but you were not pleased.
Spoiled in the luxury of Alexander's house   1020
you liked foreigners to kiss the ground before your feet.
All that impressed you.
                              And now you dare to come outside,
figure fastidiously arranged, to look upon
the same air as your husband, O abominable
heart, who should walk submissively in rags of robes,   1025
shivering with anxiety, head Scythian-cropped,
your old impudence gone and modesty gained at last
by reason of your sinful life.
                              O Menelaus,
mark this, the end of my argument. Be true to your
high reputation and to Hellas. Grace both, and kill   1030

Helen. Thus make it the custom toward all womankind
hereafter, that the price of adultery is death.

Chorus

Menelaus, keep the ancestral honor of your house.
Punish your wife, and purge away from Greece the stigma
on women. You shall seem great even to your enemies. 1035

Menelaus

All you have said falls into line with my own thought.
This woman left my household for a stranger's bed
of her own free will, and all this talk of Aphrodite
is for pure show. Away, and face the stones of the mob.
Atone for the long labors of the Achaeans in 1040
the brief act of dying, and know your penance for my shame.

(*Helen drops before him and embraces his knees.*)

Helen

No, by your knees! I am not guilty of the mind's
infection, which the gods sent. Do not kill! Have pity!

Hecuba

Be true to the memory of all your friends she murdered.
It is for them and for their children that I plead. 1045

(*Menelaus pushes Helen away.*)

Menelaus

Enough, Hecuba. I am not listening to her now.
I speak to my servants: see that she is taken away
to where the ships are beached. She will make the voyage home.

Hecuba

But let her not be put in the same ship with you.

Menelaus

What can you mean? That she is heavier than she was? 1050

Hecuba

A man in love once never is out of love again.

Menelaus

Sometimes; when the beloved's heart turns false to him.
Yet it shall be as you wish. She shall not be allowed

in the same ship I sail in. This was well advised.
And once in Argos she must die the vile death earned   ·   1055
by her vile life, and be an example to all women
to live temperately. This is not the easier way;
and yet her execution will tincture with fear
the lust of women even more depraved than she.

(Helen is led out, Menelaus following.)

Chorus
    Thus, O Zeus, you betrayed all   1060
    to the Achaeans: your temple
    in Ilium, your misted altar,
    the flame of the clotted sacraments,
    the smoke of the skying incense,
    Pergamum the hallowed,   1065
    the ivied ravines of Ida, washed
    by the running snow. The utter
    peaks that surprise the sun bolts,
    shining and primeval place of divinity.   1070

    Gone are your sacrifices, the choirs'
    glad voices singing to the gods
    night long, deep into darkness;
    gone the images, gold on wood
    laid, the twelves of the sacred moons,   1075
    the magic Phrygian number.
    Can it be, can it be, my lord, you have forgotten
    from your throne high in heaven's
    bright air, my city which is ruined
    and the flame storm that broke it?   1080

    O my dear, my husband,
    O wandering ghost
    unwashed, unburied; the sea hull must carry me   1085
    in the flash of its wings' speed
    to Argos, city of horses, where
    the stone walls built by giants invade the sky.   1090
    The multitudes of our children stand

clinging to the gates and cry through their tears.
And one girl weeps:
"O Mother, the Achaeans take me away
lonely from your eyes
to the black ship
where the oars dip surf   1095
toward Salamis the blessed,
or the peak between two seas
where Pelops' hold
keeps the gates at the Isthmus."

Oh that as Menelaus' ship   1100
makes way through the mid-sea
the bright pronged spear immortal of thunder might smash it
far out in the Aegaean,
as in tears, in bondage to Hellas   1105
I am cut from my country;
as she holds the golden mirror
in her hands, girls' grace,
she, God's daughter.
Let him never come home again, to a room in Laconia   1110
and the hearth of his fathers;
never more to Pitana's streets
and the bronze gates of the Maiden;
since he forgave his shame
and the vile marriage, the sorrows   1115
of great Hellas and the land
watered by Simois.

> (*Talthybius returns. His men carry, laid on the shield of
> Hector, the body of Astyanax.*)

But see!
Now evils multiply in our land.
Behold, O pitiful wives
of the Trojans. This is Astyanax,   1120
dead, dashed without pity from the walls, and borne
by the Danaans, who murdered him.

Talthybius
    Hecuba, one last vessel of Achilles' son
    remains, manned at the oar sweeps now, to carry back
    to the shores of Phthiotis his last spoils of war.   1125
    Neoptolemus himself has put to sea. He heard
    news of old Peleus in difficulty and the land
    invaded by Acastus, son of Pelias.
    Such news put speed above all pleasure of delay.
    So he is gone, and took with him Andromache,   1130
    whose lamentations for her country and farewells
    to Hector's tomb as she departed brought these tears
    crowding into my eyes. And she implored that you
    bury this dead child, your own Hector's son, who died
    flung from the battlements of Troy. She asked as well   1135
    that the bronze-backed shield, terror of the Achaeans once,
    when the boy's father slung its defense across his side,
    be not taken to the hearth of Peleus, nor the room
    where the slain child's Andromache must be a bride
    once more, to waken memories by its sight, but used   1140
    in place of the cedar coffin and stone-chambered tomb
    for the boy's burial. He shall be laid in your arms
    to wrap the body about with winding sheets, and flowers,
    as well as you can, out of that which is left to you.
    Since she is gone. Her master's speed prevented her   1145
    from giving the rites of burial to her little child.

    The rest of us, once the corpse is laid out, and earth
    is piled above it, must raise the mast tree, and go.
    Do therefore quickly everything that you must do.
    There is one labor I myself have spared you. As   1150
    we forded on our way here Scamander's running water,
    I washed the body and made clean the wounds. I go
    now, to break ground and dig the grave for him, that my
    work be made brief, as yours must be, and our tasks end
    together, and the ships be put to sea, for home.   1155

Hecuba

Lay down the circled shield of Hector on the ground:
a hateful thing to look at; it means no love to me.

(*Talthybius and his escort leave. Two soldiers wait.*)

Achaeans! All your strength is in your spears, not in
the mind. What were you afraid of, that it made you kill
this child so savagely? That Troy, which fell, might be   1160
raised from the ground once more? Your strength meant
    nothing, then.
When Hector's spear was fortunate, and numberless
strong hands were there to help him, we were still destroyed.
Now when the city is fallen and the Phrygians slain,
this baby terrified you? I despise the fear   1165
which is pure terror in a mind unreasoning.

O darling child, how wretched was this death. You might
have fallen fighting for your city, grown to man's
age, and married, and with the king's power like a god's,
and died happy, if there is any happiness here.   1170
But no. You grew to where you could see and learn, my child,
yet your mind was not old enough to win advantage
of fortune. How wickedly, poor boy, your fathers' walls,
Apollo's handiwork, have crushed your pitiful head
tended and trimmed to ringlets by your mother's hand,   1175
and the face she kissed once, where the brightness now is blood
shining through the torn bones—too horrible to say more.
O little hands, sweet likenesses of Hector's once,
now you lie broken at the wrists before my feet;
and mouth beloved whose words were once so confident,   1180
you are dead; and all was false, when you would lean across
my bed, and say: "Mother, when you die I will cut
my long hair in your memory, and at your grave
bring companies of boys my age, to sing farewell."
It did not happen; now I, a homeless, childless, old   1185
woman must bury your poor corpse, which is so young.
Alas for all the tendernesses, my nursing care,

and all your slumbers gone. What shall the poet say,
what words will he inscribe upon your monument?
Here lies a little child the Argives killed, because   1190
they were afraid of him. That? The epitaph of Greek shame.
You will not win your father's heritage, except
for this, which is your coffin now: the brazen shield.

O shield, who guarded the strong shape of Hector s arm:
the bravest man of all, who wore you once, is dead.   1195
How sweet the impression of his body on your sling,
and at the true circle of your rim the stain of sweat
where in the grind of his many combats Hector leaned
his chin against you, and the drops fell from his brow!

Take up your work now; bring from what is left some robes   1200
to wrap the tragic dead. The gods will not allow us
to do it right. But let him have what we can give.

That mortal is a fool who, prospering, thinks his life
has any strong foundation; since our fortune's course
of action is the reeling way a madman takes,   1205
and no one person is ever happy all the time.

> (*Hecuba's handmaidens bring out from the shelter a basket of*
> *robes and ornaments. During the scene which follows,*
> *the body of Astyanax is being made ready for burial.*)

Chorus
　Here are your women, who bring you from the Trojan spoils
　such as is left, to deck the corpse for burial.

Hecuba
　O child, it is not for victory in riding, won
　from boys your age, not archery—in which acts our people   1210
　take pride, without driving competition to excess—
　that your sire's mother lays upon you now these treasures
　from what was yours before; though now the accursed of God,
　Helen, has robbed you, she who has destroyed as well
　the life in you, and brought to ruin all our house.   1215

Chorus

    My heart,
    you touched my heart, you who were once
    a great lord in my city.

Hecuba

    These Phrygian robes' magnificence you should have worn
    at your marriage to some princess uttermost in pride
    in all the East, I lay upon your body now.   1220
    And you, once so victorious and mother of
    a thousand conquests, Hector's huge beloved shield:
    here is a wreath for you, who die not, yet are dead
    with this body; since it is better far to honor you
    than the armor of Odysseus the wicked and wise.   1225

Chorus

    Ah me.
    Earth takes you, child;
    our tears of sorrow.
    Cry aloud, our mother.

Hecuba

                     Yes.

Chorus

    The dirge of the dead.

Hecuba

                 Ah me.   1230

Chorus

    Evils never to be forgotten.

Hecuba

    I will bind up your wounds with bandages, and be
    your healer: a wretched one, in name alone, no use.
    Among the dead your father will take care of you.

Chorus

    Rip, tear your faces with hands   1235
    that beat like oars.
    Alas.

Hecuba

Dear women. . . .

Chorus

Hecuba, speak to us. We are yours. What did you cry aloud?

Hecuba

The gods meant nothing except to make life hard for me,   1240
and of all cities they chose Troy to hate. In vain
we sacrificed. And yet had not the very hand
of God gripped and crushed this city deep in the ground,
we should have disappeared in darkness, and not given
a theme for music, and the songs of men to come.   1245
You may go now, and hide the dead in his poor tomb;
he has those flowers that are the right of the underworld.
I think it makes small difference to the dead, if they
are buried in the tokens of luxury. All this
is an empty glorification left for those who live.   1250

(*The soldiers take up and carry away the body*
of Astyanax.)

Chorus

Sad mother, whose hopes were so huge
for your life. They are broken now.
Born to high blessedness
and a lordly line
your death was horror.   1255

But see, see
on the high places of Ilium
the torchflares whirling in the hands
of men. For Troy
some ultimate agony.

(*Talthybius comes back, with numerous men.*)

Talthybius

I call to the captains who have orders to set fire   1260
to the city of Priam: shield no longer in the hand
the shining flame. Let loose the fire upon it. So

with the citadel of Ilium broken to the ground
we can take leave of Troy, in gladness, and go home.

I speak to you, too, for my orders include this. 1265
Children of Troy, when the lords of the armament sound
the high echoing crash of the trumpet call, then go
to the ships of the Achaeans, to be taken away
from this land. And you, unhappiest and aged woman,
go with them. For Odysseus' men are here, to whom 1270
enslaved the lot exiles you from your native land.

Hecuba

Ah, wretched me. So this is the unhappy end
and goal of all the sorrows I have lived. I go
forth from my country and a city lit with flames.
Come, aged feet; make one last weary struggle, that I 1275
may hail my city in its affliction. O Troy, once
so huge over all Asia in the drawn wind of pride,
your very name of glory shall be stripped away.
They are burning you, and us they drag forth from our land
enslaved. O gods! Do I call upon those gods for help? 1280
I cried to them before now, and they would not hear.
Come then, hurl ourselves into the pyre. Best now
to die in the flaming ruins of our fathers' house!

Talthybius

Unhappy creature, ecstatic in your sorrows! Men,
take her, spare not. She is Odysseus' property. 1285
You have orders to deliver her into his hands.

Hecuba

O sorrow.
Cronion, Zeus, lord of Phrygia,
prince of our house, have you seen
the dishonor done to the seed of Dardanus? 1290

Chorus

He has seen, but the great city
is a city no more, it is gone. There is no Troy.

Hecuba

O sorrow.

Ilium flares.   1295

The chambers of Pergamum take fire,

the citadel and the wall's high places.

Chorus

Our city fallen to the spear

fades as smoke winged in the sky.

halls hot in the swept fire   1300

and the fierce lances.

Hecuba

O soil where my children grew.

Chorus

Alas.

Hecuba

O children, hear me; it is your mother who calls.

Chorus

They are dead you cry to. This is a dirge.

Hecuba

I lean my old body against the earth   1305

and both hands beat the ground.

Chorus

I kneel to the earth, take up

the cry to my own dead,

poor buried husband.

Hecuba

We are taken, dragged away

Chorus

                            a cry of pain, pain   1310

Hecuba

under the slave's roof

Chorus

                        away from my country.

Hecuba
Priam, my Priam. Dead
graveless, forlorn,
you know not what they have done to me.

Chorus
Now dark, holy death   1315
in the brutal butchery closed his eyes.

Hecuba
O gods' house, city beloved

Chorus
alas

Hecuba
you are given the red flame and the spear's iron.

Chorus
You will collapse to the dear ground and be nameless.

Hecuba
Ash as the skyward smoke wing   1320
piled will blot from my sight the house where I lived once.

Chorus
Lost shall be the name on the land,
all gone, perished. Troy, city of sorrow,
is there no longer.

Hecuba
Did you see, did you hear?

Chorus
                        The crash of the citadel.   1325

Hecuba
The earth shook, riven

Chorus
                  to engulf the city.

Hecuba
O
shaking, tremulous limbs,

this is the way. Forward:
into the slave's life.   1330

Chorus
   Mourn for the ruined city, then go away
   to the ships of the Achaeans.

> (*Hecuba is led away, and all go out, leaving
> the stage empty.*)

ION

Translated by R. F. Willetts

INTRODUCTION TO *ION*

THE *Ion* can be fairly certainly assigned, on stylistic and metrical grounds, to the decade 420–410 B.C. There is no conclusive evidence for a more exact date within this period.

Creusa was the daughter of Erechtheus, the autochthonous king of Athens. While still a girl, she was seduced by Apollo and gave birth to a son whom she exposed from fear of her parents. She naturally supposed that the child had died. But, unknown to her, Apollo sent Hermes to take the child to Delphi and leave him beside the temple. There he was found by the prophetess, who brought him up. He eventually became a steward in the temple. Knowing nothing of the circumstances of his birth, he lives a sheltered life and is happy in the service of the god. In the meantime his mother has married Xuthus. He, though a foreigner, won his bride as a reward for his services to Athens in war. Though long married, they are childless. They have therefore decided to come to Delphi to consult the god about their chances of having children.

Such is the situation at the opening of the play. It arose from an old wrong, the seduction of Creusa by Apollo. It lends itself to development in a number of different ways. The wrong can be righted and Athens glorified by accepting Ion's divine birth as a mark of favor to the Ionian tribes. Or the romantic can be rejected in favor of a more realistic approach. Euripides was sometimes romantic, more often realistic, in his treatment of myths. Here he chose to handle the theme realistically and was preoccupied with the human problem it presented. He weaves the strands of the Ion legend together to form the framework outlined above. He then tears from the story its mythological and supernatural pretensions—at least until Athene appears as *dea ex machina*. Here, at first sight, it seems that the playwright welcomes her with gratitude to supply a ready-made solution for his tangled plot.

The essence of the realist method in this play lies in the double-edged treatment of mythology. Euripides accepts Apollo as the divine lover of Creusa and then invests him with human attributes. In consequence, Apollo emerges in very poor light as a barbarian god whose ethics are shattered by the probings of a civilized and skeptical mind. This exposure is achieved not only by Creusa's intense denunciation of the god in a moment of high climax in the unfolding of the intricate plot. It is more subtly managed through the impact of the whole action upon the boy, Ion. Perhaps the chief merit of this well-designed play is the careful study of Ion's development, the revelation of the changes brought about by the abrupt contact of youthful, cloistered virtue with worldliness. At times we may suspect that the boy grows up too quickly—not so quickly, however, that he becomes a cynic: though he learns with rapidity, he also learns ingenuously. As he becomes more and more disturbed, and therefore more and more disturbing, to his initial charm are added self-confidence and strength of will.

As the plot is presented, Ion is foisted as a son upon Xuthus by the oracle. This leads to the attempt of the mother to kill her son. When this is foiled there follows the further attempt of the son to kill his mother. The rest of the play falls into two parts—the cleverly contrived recognition scene between mother and son and the appearance of Athene as *dea ex machina*.

To accept the resolution of the play at its face value is impossible if we are to believe that there is any serious purpose behind it. Until the end we have no doubts that Euripides is, in fact, dealing with an important theme in earnest. At the end we are likely to feel that our emotions have been cheated; for the explanations of the goddess seem paltry and inconsistent with the dramatic quality and the seriousness of all that has gone before. The contrast is so marked that the play cannot be easily accepted as a tragicomic fairy tale with a well-knit, tense plot and a happy ending, designed to extol the Apolline origin of the Athenian race. The poignant dramatic structure, we feel, must not be reduced to the level of a preface to a pamphlet, even if delivered by an Olympian.

In other words, there is a critical problem to be solved here. Now the "rationalizing" view of the play, associated particularly with A. W. Verrall, had the merit of recognizing that this problem exists.

Verrall agreed with the argument that the *Ion* is an attack upon
Delphi and must be interpreted in this way; that the oracle delivered
to Xuthus, like the recognition scene between Creusa and Ion, is a
Delphian fraud, the attribution of Ion to Apollo and Creusa being
due to a change of tactics following upon Creusa's confession and
denunciation of Apollo.

But this "rationalizing" solution ignores a most important point.
Creusa, even when Ion takes her aside in confidence and suggests the
possibility, will not admit that her lover was a mortal man. The
whole design of the play depends on the assumption that Apollo
seduced Creusa. Are the design and the assumption sustained
throughout? Let us examine the last two scenes with this query in
mind.

As Ion and the crowd advance threateningly toward Creusa, after
she has been discovered in refuge at the altar, the Pythian priestess
enters from the temple, carrying a cradle bound with fillets of wool
resembling those on the altar. She had kept the cradle in which she
had found Ion, together with his swaddling clothes and ornaments,
and now gives them to him in case he should find a clue to his
mother's identity in Athens or elsewhere. Ion examines the cradle
with great interest, marveling at the freshness of its fastenings. On
the "rationalist" view this would have been part of the fraud per-
petrated by the Delphians, since Euripides could not have intended
such magical hocus-pocus to be taken seriously: that would have
been inconsistent with his "rationalism." But Euripides is consist-
ently irrational in such respects in other plays; though inconsistency
is one of his strongest characteristics as a playwright.

When Ion unties the fillets, Creusa recognizes the cradle, is over-
whelmed for the moment and then rushes from the altar to embrace
him, prepared to risk death, and greets him as her child. He supposes
she is playing a trick on him, orders the guards to seize her, and then
decides on a better method. He will test her knowledge of the con-
tents of the cradle. But Creusa answers all his questions. Ion is convinced she is his mother. In the joy of her discovery all thought of
Xuthus is obliterated. Her son has brought her her personal triumph.
As she had tried to murder him as a menace, so now she welcomes

ION

segION »

him as the savior of her house. The stigma of childlessness is removed together with the memory of Xuthus as the partner of her unhappiness. He has no mention in her triumphant outburst.

Ion puts an end to this rapture by asking for his father to be there to share their happiness. Creusa is again obliged to describe the seduction by Apollo. Ion is guarded in his reception of the story, though his sympathy with his mother as she describes her suffering is spontaneously generous. He can credit the story—with reservations. This is clear when, after making some platitudinous remarks about the workings of providence, intended for the Chorus and others on the stage, he draws his mother aside and puts the question that is uppermost in his mind. Is Apollo being made into a convenient scapegoat?

This is a crucial passage where the "rationalist" explanation breaks down. Ion makes a natural assumption. It demands a truthful answer. There have been enough complications in the plot. Let us suppose that Creusa had agreed with his suggestion. She would presumably have made some confession of an intrigue in her youth. Ion would then have asked the reason for the oracle's deception in giving him to Xuthus as his son. The fraud which the "rationalizers" are anxious to prove would have been most obvious and the play would become more of an open attack upon Delphi than a criticism of Olympian morals. Creusa and Ion might then have agreed, for the sake of convenience, to leave Xuthus in blissful ignorance of the facts, the happy ending would be dramatically justified, the purpose of propaganda achieved, and Athene could have predicted Ion's future without having to make lame excuses for Apollo. The main objection to all this is that, since no one was aware of the birth and exposure of the child except the mother, there was no reason to put any blame upon Apollo. Yet Euripides purposely adopts that version of the story.

Instead, what happens? Creusa vehemently denies any suggestion of deceit. The play proceeds and still gains its effects from the assumption that Apollo was the father. The characters still continue to judge him by human standards. For Ion immediately asks why Apollo should give his own son to Xuthus, with the plain falsehood that he was the father. Creusa, now quite happy in the possession of her son, is content to let moral problems go by the board. Apollo, she says, practiced the deceit out of kindness to Ion. But Ion is not satisfied. He has already received some shocks to his beliefs. His only wish now is to decide finally whether Apollo is a sham:

> But, mother, does Apollo tell the truth,
> Or is the oracle false? With some good reason
> That question troubles me.

Creusa offers the same explanation again, but Ion's question "cannot be so lightly answered." He is about to enter the temple to ask the oracle if Apollo is his father when Athene appears. She begins by saying that Apollo did not care to come, since some criticism of his previous conduct might be expected. This answer to Creusa's earlier challenge is intentionally farcical. Apollo now becomes contemptible. Ion is saved the trouble of consulting the oracle. Athene assures him that Apollo is really his father. The legend is preserved to the end. But Ion's question is ignored. The answer is too obvious.

Athene's final remarks are all the more ironic because redundant. They are an appeal to faith, and Euripides has done his best to destroy the basis of faith. Even now Apollo can go merrily on from one deceit to another. Xuthus is not to know the truth, and Apollo makes Creusa and Ion partners in his falsehood. Only Athene, Hermes, and Creusa seem satisfied that Apollo "has managed all things well." Certainly no reader of the play can be. But Creusa, at least, may be pardoned for grasping her long-awaited reward without too much questioning.

Athene serves a double function. As in other plays of Euripides with a *deus ex machina*, she commemorates the foundation of a hero-cult and prophesies future Athenian history. At the same time, by uttering her divine commonplaces, she adds nothing to our knowledge but fits in with the dramatic purpose of the play. Before her appearance Apollo had still some chance to justify himself. After it, he retains no shred of dignity.

ION

CHARACTERS

Hermes

Ion

Chorus (Creusa's attendants)

Creusa

Xuthus

Old Man

A Servant

Pythian priestess

Athene

ION

Before the temple of Apollo at Delphi, just before sunrise.

(Enter Hermes.)

Hermes

    Atlas, who wears on back of bronze the ancient
    Abode of gods in heaven, had a daughter
    Whose name was Maia, born of a goddess:
    She lay with Zeus and bore me, Hermes, servant
    Of the immortals. I have come here to Delphi   5
    Where Phoebus sits at earth's mid-center, gives
    His prophecies to men, and passes judgment
    On what is happening now and what will come.
      For in the famous city of the Greeks
    Called after Pallas of the Golden Spear,
    Phoebus compelled Erechtheus' daughter Creusa   10
    To take him as her lover—in that place
    Below Athene's hill whose northern scarp
    The Attic lords have named the Long Rocks.
    Her father, by the god's own wish, did not
    Suspect her, and she carried her child in secret.   15
    And when the time had come, her son was born,
    Inside the palace. Then she took the child
    To the same cave where she had lain with Phoebus,
    And in a wicker cradle there exposed
    Him to his death. She kept an ancient custom   20
    Begun in Athens when Athene placed
    By Erichthonius, son of Earth, two snakes
    As guardians, when the daughters of Aglaurus
    Were given charge of him.
                      And so Creusa tied   25
    To him whatever girlish ornaments
    She had, before she left him to his death.
    My brother Phoebus then made this request:

"You know Athene's city well," he said,
"Now will you journey to the earth-born people
Of glorious Athens? There, inside a cave
A newborn child is hidden. Take the child,
His cradle, and his swaddling clothes and bring
Them to my oracle at Delphi, where
They must be left before the temple entrance.
I will arrange the rest. The child is mine."
   I did as Loxias my brother wished,
Took up the wicker cradle, brought it here,
Setting it on the temple steps before
I opened it, so that someone might see
The child. Now when the sun began to ride
In heaven, the prophetess was entering
The holy shrine. Her eyes were drawn toward
The helpless child. Astonished that a girl
Of Delphi should dare to cast her secret child
Before Apollo's temple, she would have taken it
Outside the sacred precinct, but her pity
Expelled the cruel impulse—and the god
Designed to keep his son within his house.
And so she took the child and reared him,
Not knowing who his mother was, or that
Apollo was his father; while the child
Has never known his parents. His childhood home
Has been about the altars where he played
And wandered. But when he was fully grown,
The Delphians appointed him their steward,
The trusted guardian of Apollo's gold.
And he has lived a holy life until
This day, within the shrine.
                Creusa, whose son
He is, has married Xuthus. This is how
The marriage occurred. A war was surging high
Between Chalcidians of Euboea and Athens,
Whose ally, Xuthus, helped to end the strife.

30

35

40

45

50

55

60

Though he was not a native, but Achaean,
Son of Aeolus, son of Zeus, the prize
He won was marriage to Creusa. But
In all these years no children have been born. 65
Desire for children is now bringing them
To Apollo's shrine. Apollo seems indifferent,
But he controls their fate and guides them here.
When Xuthus comes before the shrine, the god
Will give him his own son, declaring Xuthus 70
The father. Thus the boy shall be received
Into his mother's house, made known to her.
And while Apollo's intrigue is kept secret,
His son may have what is his due. Moreover,
Apollo will bestow on him the name
Of Ion, make that name renowned through Greece 75
As founder of ancient cities.
                    Now, because
I wish to see this young boy's destiny
Complete, I shall conceal myself within
These laurel groves. This is Apollo's son,
Who comes here now, with branches of bay, to make
The portals bright before the temple. And I
Will be the first of all the gods to call 80
Him by his future name of—Ion.

(*The central doors of the temple open, and Ion comes out with
a group of Delphian servants. He is wearing a brightly colored
tunic and cloak, and on his head is a wreath of bay leaves.
He carries a bow and arrow, symbol of his service to
Apollo, which is to have a more practical purpose later
in the scene. The two peaks of Parnassus which
overlook the temple have caught the first rays of
the dawn, and Ion points to them as he
begins to speak.*)

Ion

Look, now the sun's burning chariot comes
Casting his light on the earth.

Banned by his flame, the stars flee
To the awful darkness of space.   85
The untrodden peaks of Parnassus,
Kindling to flame, receive for mankind
The disk of the day.

   The smoke of unwatered myrrh drifts
To the top of the temple.   90
The Delphian priestess sits on the
Sacred tripod chanting to the Greeks
Echoes of Apollo's voice.

   You Delphians, attendants of Phoebus,
Go down to Castalia's silvery eddies: 95
When you have bathed in its holy dews,
Return to the temple.
Let your lips utter no words
Of ill-omen, may your tongues
Be gracious and gentle to those who   100
Come to the oracle.

   As for myself, mine is the task
I have always done since my childhood.
With these branches of bay and these sacred
Garlands I will brighten Apollo's
Portals, cleanse the floor with   105
Sprinklings of water,
Put to flight with my arrows the birds
Who foul the offerings.
Since I have neither mother nor father,
I revere the temple of Phoebus   110
Where I have lived.

Come, fresh-blooming branch
Of lovely laurel,
With which I sweep clean
The precinct below the shrine,   115
Sprung from the eternal garden
Where the sacred spring sends
A welling, never failing stream

From the myrtle grove
To water the sacred leaves,   120
Leaves I brush over his fane,
Every day serving with my daily task
When the sun's swift wing appears.

O Healer! O Healer!   125
My blessing! My blessing!
O Leto's son!

Fair, fair is the labor,
O Phoebus, which
I am doing for you,
Honoring the prophetic place.   130
I have a glorious task:
To set my hands to serve
Not a man but the immortals.
I will never weary
Over my pious tasks.   135
I praise him who feeds me, Phoebus
My father—his love deserves the name,
Phoebus, lord of the temple.   140

O Healer! O Healer!
My blessing! My blessing!
O Leto's son!

Now I have finished my sweeping
With my broom of bay,   145
I will pour from golden bowls
Water risen from the earth,
Drawn from the spring
Of Castalia.
Myself holy and chaste, I can
Cast the lustral water.   150
Always thus may I serve Phoebus,
Service without end—
Or an end come with good issue.
    Look! Look!

Here come the birds already,
Leaving their nests on Parnassus.   155
Keep away from the cornices
And the gold-decked abode.
I will strike you again with my arrows,
You herald of Zeus,
Though your beak is strong,
Surpassing the other birds.   160
Here sails another to the temple steps,
A swan.—Take to another place
Your red shining feet.
You may have your music,
But Apollo's lyre will not save you
At all from my bow,   165
Turn your wings,
Speed on to the lake of Delos.
If you do not obey,
You will raise, and in blood,
That clear-toned song.
    Look! Look!   170
What is this other bird here on its way?
Is it going to build in the cornice
A nest of dry twigs for its young?
The twang of my bow will prevent it.
Go, I tell you and rear
Your young in the eddies of Alpheus   175
Or the Isthmian grove,
Without fouling the offerings
And Apollo's shrine.
Yet I scruple to kill you
Who announce to mankind
The will of the gods.   180
But I will bend to the labors
Of my devotion,
Never ceasing to honor him
Who gives me life.

(Ion goes out. The Delphian servants enter in silence and per-
form a sacrifice on the altar in front of the temple. After the
sacrifice the Chorus, young girl servants of Creusa, enter.
They pass up and down, excitedly admiring the
temple buildings.)

Chorus

Not only in holy Athens after all
Are there courts of the gods   185
With fair columns, and homage paid
To Apollo who protects the streets.
Here too on this temple
Of Leto's son shows
The bright-eyed beauty of twin façades.

Look, look at this: Zeus's son   190
Is killing the Lernaean Hydra
With a golden sickle,
Look there, my dear.

Yes—and near him another is raising
On high a flaming torch.   195
Can it be he whose story I hear
As I sit at my weaving,
Iolaus the shield-bearer,
Companion of Heracles,
Whom he helped to endure his labors?   200

And look at this one
On a horse with wings.
He is killing the mighty three-bodied
Fire-breathing monster.

My eyes dart everywhere.   205
See! The battle of the giants
On the marble walls.

Yes we are looking.

Can you see her, brandishing
Her Gorgon shield against Enceladus—?   210

I can see my goddess Pallas Athene.

Oh! The terrible thunderbolt
With fire at each end which Zeus holds
Ready to throw.

Yes I see. Raging Mimas
Is burnt up in the flames.   215

And Bacchus, the boisterous god,
With unwarlike wand of ivy is killing
Another of Earth's giant sons.

                    (*Ion enters through the central doors of the temple.*)

Chorus Leader
    You there by the temple,
    May we with naked feet   220
    Pass into this sanctuary?

Ion
    You may not, strangers.

Chorus Leader
    Perhaps you would tell me—?

Ion
    Tell me, what do you want?

Chorus Leader
    Is it true that Apollo's temple
    Really contains the world's center?

Ion
    Yes, wreathed in garlands, flanked by Gorgons.

Chorus Leader
    That is the story we have heard.   225

Ion
    If you have offered sacrificial food
    In front of the temple, and you have a question
    For Apollo to answer, come to the altar steps.

But do not pass into the inner shrine
Unless you have slaughtered a sheep.

Chorus Leader

  I understand.
  We are not for transgressing Apollo's law.   230
  The outside charms us enough.

Ion

  Look where you please at what is lawful.

Chorus Leader

  Our masters have allowed us
  To look over this sanctuary of Apollo.

Ion

  In whose house do you serve?

Chorus Leader

  The dwelling place of Pallas   235
  Is the house of our masters.
  But the person you ask about is here.

                        (Enter Creusa.)

Ion

  Whoever you may be, you are a noble,
  Your looks reveal your character: by looks
  Nobility is often to be judged.   240
  But?—You surprise me—why, your eyes are closed,
  That noble face is wet with tears—and now!
  When you have seen Apollo's holy temple.
  What reason can there be for your distraction?
  Where others are glad to see the sanctuary,   245
  Your eyes are filled with tears.

Creusa

  That you should be surprised about my tears
  Is not ill-bred. But when I saw this temple,
  I measured an old memory again,   250
  My mind elsewhere, though I stand here.

(*aside*) Unhappy women! Where shall we appeal
For justice when the injustice of power
Is our destruction?

Ion

What is the cause of this strange melancholy?   255

Creusa

Nothing. Now I have loosed my shaft I shall
Be silent, and you will not think of it.

Ion

But tell me who you are, your family,
Your country. And what is you name?

Creusa

Creusa is my name, Erechtheus' daughter,   260
And Athens is my native land.

Ion

A famous city and a noble race!
How fortunate you are!

Creusa

Yes, fortunate in that—but nothing else.

Ion

There is a story told—can that be true?   265

Creusa

But tell me what you want to know.

Ion

Your father's ancestor sprang from the earth?

Creusa

Yes, Erichthonius—the glory is no help.

Ion

Athene really took him from the earth?

Creusa

Into her virgin arms, though not her son.   270

Ion

And then she gave him as we see in paintings—

Creusa

To Cecrops' daughters, who were to keep him hidden.

Ion

I have been told they opened the cradle.

Creusa

And died for it. The rocks were stained with blood.

Ion

Oh. (*pauses*)
The other story? Is that true or not?   275

Creusa

Which one is that?—I have time to answer.

Ion

Well, did your father sacrifice your sisters?

Creusa

He had the courage. They were killed for Athens.

Ion

How was it you were saved, the only one?

Creusa

I was a baby in my mother's arms.   280

Ion

And was your father buried in a chasm?

Creusa

The sea-god's trident blows destroyed him.

Ion

There is a place there which is called Long Rocks?

Creusa

Oh, why ask that?—You are reminding me.—

Ion

The lightning-fire of Phoebus honors it.   285

Creusa

Vain honor. I wish I had never seen it.

Ion

Why do you hate a place he dearly loves?

Creusa

No matter.—But I know its secret shame.—

Ion

And what Athenian became your husband?

Creusa

My husband is no citizen of Athens.   290

Ion

Who then? He must have been of noble birth.

Creusa

Xuthus, the son of Aeolus and Zeus.

Ion

A stranger. How then could he marry you?

Creusa

A neighboring land of Athens is Euboea—

Ion

Which has a sea for boundary they say.   295

Creusa

—Which Athens conquered with the help of Xuthus.

Ion

The ally came, and you were his reward?

Creusa

Dowry of war, the prize won with his spear.

Ion

And have you come alone or with your husband?

Creusa

With him. But he stayed at Trophonius' shrine.   300

Ion

To see it or consult the oracle?

Creusa
To ask the same as he will ask of Phoebus.

Ion
Is it about your country's crops—or children?

Creusa
Though married long ago, we have no children.

Ion
No children? You have never had a child?   305

Creusa
Apollo knows my childlessness.

Ion
Ah! That misfortune cancels all your blessings.

Creusa
And who are you? Your mother must be happy!

Ion
I am what I am called, Apollo's slave.

Creusa
A city's votive gift or sold by someone?   310

Ion
I only know that I am called Apollo's.

Creusa
So now it is my turn to pity you!

Ion
Because my parents are unknown to me.

Creusa
You live inside the temple? Or at home?

Ion
Apollo's home is mine, wherever I sleep.   315

Creusa
And did you come here as a child?

Ion
A child, they say who seem to know.

Creusa

What Delphian woman suckled you?

Ion

No breast fed me. But she who reared me.—

Creusa

Yes, who, poor child?

(*aside*) A sorrow like my own.   320

Ion

The prophetess, I think of her as mother.

Creusa

But what supported you as you grew up?

Ion

The altars and the visitors who came.

Creusa

And your unhappy mother! Who was she then?

Ion

My birth perhaps marked her betrayal.   325

Creusa

You are not poor? Your robes are fine enough.

Ion

These robes belong to him, the god I serve.

Creusa

But have you never tried to find your parents?

Ion

How can I when I have no clues to guide?

Creusa

Ah yes. (*pause*)

Another suffered as your mother did.   330

Ion

Who was she then? If she would help me in my grief!   331

Creusa

On her behalf I came before my husband.   332

Ion
Why did you come? Tell me and I will help.   333

Creusa
I have a friend—who says—she lay with Phoebus.   338

Ion
Not Phoebus and a mortal woman. No!

Creusa
And had a child unknown to her own father.   340

Ion
She is ashamed to own some man's betrayal.

Creusa
But she says not. Her life has been most wretched.

Ion
Why, if her lover was a god?

Creusa
She put from out the house the child she had.

Ion
Where is the child? Is it alive?   345

Creusa
I have come here to ask, for no one knows.

Ion
If he is dead, how did he die?

Creusa
Killed by wild beasts, she thinks.

Ion
What reason could she have for thinking so?

Creusa
She could not find him when she went again.   350

Ion
But were there drops of blood upon the ground?

Creusa
She says not, though her search was careful.

Ion

And how long is it since the child was killed?

Creusa

He would have been your age by now.

Ion

Apollo is unjust. She has my pity.   355

Creusa

For she has never had another child.

> (*Pause as Ion reflects. He is still unwilling
> to believe Apollo guilty.*)

Ion

Supposing Phoebus reared him in secret?

Creusa

To keep that pleasure for himself is wrong.

Ion (*sighs*)

Ah! This misfortune echoes my own grief.

Creusa

And some unhappy mother misses you.   360

Ion

Do not revive the grief I had forgotten.

Creusa

No.—Then you will see to my request?

Ion

But do you know where that request is faulty?

Creusa

What is not faulty for that wretched woman?

Ion

Will Phoebus tell the secret he wants to hide?   365

Creusa

If oracles are open to all Greeks.

Ion

Do not press him to reveal his shame.

Creusa

His shame means suffering to her!

Ion

No one will give this oracle to you.
Convicted of evil here inside his own temple,   370
Apollo would justly take vengeance on
His prophet. Think no more of it: avoid
A question which the god himself opposes.
This foolishness we should commit in trying
By any means to force reluctant answers,   375
Whether by slaying sheep before the altar
Or taking omens from the flight of birds.
The benefits we win by force against
Their will are never blessed. We only profit
By what the gods give with their blessing.   380

Chorus Leader

The woes assailing human life are many,
The forms of woe diverse. And happiness
Is rare and rarely comes to light on man.

Creusa

                    (*Raising her hands toward the temple.*)

Apollo! Then and now unjust to her,
The absent woman whose complaints are here.   385
You did not save the child you should have saved.
A prophet, you have no answer for its mother.
But now that hope must die, because the god   390
Prevents me learning what I wish to know.
But I can see my noble husband, Xuthus,
Arriving from Trophonius' cave. He is
Quite near; I beg you, stranger, tell him nothing
Of what we have been saying. Or I may   395
Be suspect, meddling in these secret matters,
And then this story will not have the end
We have designed. For trouble is very easy
When women deal with men. Since good and bad

Are not distinguished, all of us are hated.
To this misfortune we are born.   400

                    (*Xuthus enters with servants and Delphians.*)

Xuthus

My greeting first is to the god, and then
To you my wife.

                              (*He sees she is upset.*)

                    But has my long delay
Caused you alarm?

Creusa

No. Your arrival has prevented that.
What oracle did Trophonius give about   405
Our hopes of having children?

Xuthus

He was unwilling to anticipate
Apollo's answer. But he has told me this,
That neither you nor I shall go from here
Without a child.

Creusa

O holy mother of Apollo, may   410
Our journey here end well, our dealings with
Your son have a happier issue than before!

Xuthus

So it will be! But who speaks here for Phoebus?

Ion

Sir, that is my role outside the temple—
Inside are others, near the shrine, the nobles   415
Of Delphi, chosen by lot.

Xuthus

Ah! Good. I now know all I need to know,
And shall go in. They say the victim, which
Is offered on behalf of strangers, has
Already fallen before the altar. Omens   420
Today are good, and I would like to have

My answer from the oracle. Will you,
Creusa, with laurel branches in your hand,
Go round the altars praying to the gods
That I may bring an oracle with promise
Of children from Apollo's house.

(*Xuthus enters the temple, Creusa watches him go and
speaks with her hands raised toward the temple.*)

Creusa

So it will be! So it will be!

               And now   425
If Phoebus at least amends his former wrongs,
Although his love can never be complete,
Because he is a god, I will accept
Whatever he bestows.

                               (*Exit.*)

Ion

Why does this stranger always speak in riddles,
Reproach the god with covert blasphemy?   430
Is it through love of her on whose behalf
She comes before the oracle? Perhaps
She hides a secret which she cannot tell.
But what concern have I with Erechtheus' daughter?
No, that is not my business.—I will pour
The holy water out of golden pitchers   435
Into the lustral bowls. I must confront
Apollo with his wrongs. To force a girl
Against her will and afterward betray!
To leave a child to die which has been born
In secret! No! Do not act thus. But since
You have the power, seek the virtuous path.   440
All evil men are punished by the gods.
How then can it be just for you to stand
Accused of breaking laws you have yourselves
Laid down for men? But if—here I suppose
What could not be—you gave account on earth
For wrongs which you have done to women, you,   445

Apollo and Poseidon and Zeus who rules
In heaven, payment of your penalties
Would see your temples empty, since you are
Unjust to others in pursuing pleasure
Without forethought. And justice now demands
That we should not speak ill of men if they   450
But imitate what the gods approve, but those
Who teach men their examples.

                                                    (*Exit.*)

Chorus
STROPHE

O my Athene, born
Without birth pains,
Brought forth from the head of Zeus
By Prometheus, the Titan,   455
Blessed goddess of Victory,
Take flight from the golden halls
Of Olympus, come, I entreat you,
Here to the Pythian temple,   460
Where at earth's center Apollo's shrine
Proclaims unfailing prophecy,
At the tripod where they dance and sing.
Come with Artemis, Leto's daughter,   465
Virgin goddesses both,
Holy sisters of Phoebus.
Beseech him, O maidens,
That the ancient race of Erechtheus may
At last be sure by a clear response   470
Of the blessing of children.

ANTISTROPHE

Wherever gleams bright the flame
And strength of youth,
A promise to the house of growth,
There a man has a fund   475
Of joy overflowing;

From the fathers the children will gather
Hereditary wealth, and in turn
Pass it on to their own. 480
They are a defense in adversity,
In happiness a delight,
And in war their country's shield of safety.
For myself I would choose, rather than wealth 485
Or a palace of kings, to rear
And love my own children:
Shame to him who prefers
A childless life, hateful to me.
May I cling to the life of few possessions, 490
Enriched by children.

EPODE

O haunts of Pan,
The rock flanking
The caves of the Long Cliffs,
Where the daughters of Aglaurus 495
Dance, and their feet tread
The green levels before the shrines
Of Pallas, in time to the changing
Music of the pipes, when you play, 500
O Pan, in your sunless caves,
Where a girl in misery
Bore a child to Phoebus
And exposed it, a prey for birds,
Food for wild beasts to rend, shame
Of a cruel love. 505
Our legends, our tales at the loom,
Never tell of good fortune to children
Born of a god and a mortal.

(Enter Ion from the central doors of the temple.)

Ion

Serving women who are keeping watch here at the steps 510
Of the house of sacrifice, awaiting your master,

Tell me, has Xuthus already left the sacred tripod
And the oracle, or does he still remain within,
Seeking answer to his question?

Chorus Leader

He is still inside. He has not passed this threshold yet.
But the noise the door has made shows someone is now there.   515
Look, it is my master coming.

> (*Xuthus appears from the temple. As soon as he sees Ion, he
> shows great excitement, runs to him and tries to embrace
> him. Ion, much surprised by this behavior, resists.*)

Xuthus

Son, my blessing.—It is right to greet you in this way.

Ion

Sir, my thanks. We are both well—if you are not mad.

Xuthus

Let me kiss your hand, embrace you.

Ion

Are you sane? Or can the god have made you mad somehow?   520

Xuthus

Mad, when I have found my own and want to welcome him?

Ion

Stop.—Or if you touch it, you may break Apollo's crown.

Xuthus

I will touch you. And I am no robber. You are mine.

Ion

Must I shoot this arrow first, or will you loose me now?

Xuthus

Why must you avoid me just when you have found your nearest?   525

Ion

Mad and boorish strangers are no pleasure to instruct.

Xuthus

Kill me, and then bury me. For you will kill your father.

Ion

You my father! This is fool's talk.—How can that be? No!

Xuthus

Yes.—The story which I have to tell will make it clear.

Ion

What have you to say?

Xuthus

I am your father. You are my son. 530

Ion

Who has told you this?

Xuthus

Apollo, he who reared my son.

Ion

You are your own witness.

Xuthus

But I know my oracle too.

Ion

You mistook a riddle.

Xuthus

Then my hearing must have failed.

Ion

And what is Apollo's prophecy?

Xuthus

That him I met—

Ion

Oh! A meeting? Where?

Xuthus

As I came from the temple here. 535

Ion

Yes, and what would happen to him?

Xuthus

He would be my son.

Ion

Your own son or just a gift?

Xuthus

A gift and my own son.

Ion

I was then the first you met?

Xuthus

Yes, no one else, my son.

Ion

But how strange this is!

Xuthus

I am just as amazed as you.

Ion

Well?—Who is my mother?

Xuthus

That I cannot say.   540

Ion

And Apollo?

Xuthus

Happy with this news, I did not ask.

Ion

Earth then was my mother!

Xuthus

Children do not spring up there.

Ion

How could I be yours?

Xuthus

Apollo, not I, has the answer.

Ion (*after a pause*)

Let us try another tack.

Xuthus

Yes, that will help us more.

Ion

Have you had a secret lover?

Xuthus

Yes, a youthful folly.   545

Ion
And before you were married?

Xuthus
Yes, but never afterward.

Ion
So that could be my origin?

Xuthus
Time at least agrees.

Ion
Then what am I doing here?

Xuthus
I cannot tell you that.

Ion
Here, so far away?

Xuthus
That is my puzzle too.

Ion
Have you been before to Delphi?

Xuthus
To the wine-god's torch feast. 550

Ion
You stayed with a temple steward?

Xuthus
He—there were girls of Delphi. 551

Ion
He introduced you to their rites?

Xuthus
Yes, they were Bacchanals. 552

Ion
You had drunk well?

Xuthus
I was reveling in the wine-god's feast. 553

Ion
Then that was the time.

Xuthus
> The girl perhaps exposed her child. 555

Ion (after a pause)
I am not a slave then.

Xuthus
> And you can accept a father. 556

Ion
Could I wish for better?

Xuthus
> That you might have seen before. 558

Ion
Than descent from Zeus's son?

Xuthus
> This is indeed your birthright. 559

Ion
Shall I touch my father then?

Xuthus
> Yes, have faith in the god. 560

Ion
Father—

Xuthus
> How dear is the sound of the name you have spoken!

Ion
We should both bless this day.

Xuthus
> It has brought me happiness.
> (*They embrace.*)

Ion
My dear mother! Shall I ever see your face as well?
Now, whoever you may be, I long to see you even
More. But she is dead perhaps, and I can have no hope. 565

Chorus Leader
We also share this house's happiness.
Yet I could wish my mistress too might have
The joy of children, and Erechtheus' race.

Xuthus

My son, Apollo rightly prophesied
That I should find you, and united us.   570
You found a father whom you never knew.
Your natural desire I share myself
That you will find your mother, I, in her
The woman who gave me a son. And if
We leave all that to time, perhaps we shall   575
Succeed. But end your waif's life in the temple.
Let me persuade you, come with me to Athens,
For there your father's prosperous power awaits
You, and great wealth. Though now you suffer
In one respect, you shall not have the name
Of bastard and of beggar, but highborn   580
And well endowed with wealth. But why so silent?
Why do you hold your eyes downcast? Now you have changed
Your father's joy to fear.

Ion

Things have a different face as they appear   585
Before the eyes or far away. I bless
My fortune now that I have found a father.
But, father, listen to what is in my mind:
The earth-born people of glorious Athens are said
To be no alien race. I should intrude   590
There marked by two defects, a stranger's son,
Myself a bastard. And if I remain
Obscure, with this disgrace they will account
Me nothing, nobody's son. If I aspire
To the city's helm, ambitious for a name,   595
I shall be hated by the powerless.
Authority is never without hate.
And those who have ability for power
But wisely keep their silence, are not eager
For public life, will mock my folly, blindly   600
Deserting peace for Athens' crowded fears.
And then if I invade positions which

Are filled, I shall be countered by the moves
Of those with knowledge who control affairs.
For so it always happens, father: men
Who hold the cities and their dignities   605
Above all are opposed to rivalry.

    Then, coming to another's house, a stranger,
To live with one who has no children, who
Before had you to share the sorrow—now,
Abandoned to a private grief, she will   610
Have cause for bitterness and cause enough
To hate me when I take my place as heir:
Without a child herself, she will not kindly
Regard your own. Then you must either turn
To her, betraying me, or honor me   615
And bring confusion to your house: there is
No other way. How many wives have brought
Their men to death with poison or the knife!
Then, childless, growing old, she has my pity.
For this affliction does not suit her birth.   620

    The praise of royalty itself is false—
A fair façade to hide the pain within.
What happiness or blessing has the man
Who looks askance for violence, and fear
Draws out his days? I would prefer to live   625
A happy citizen than be a king,
Compelled to have the evil as his friends,
Who must abhor the good for fear of death.
You might reply that gold outweighs all this,
The joys of wealth—no joy for me to guard   630
A fortune, hear reproaches, suffer its pains.
Let me avoid distress, win moderation.

    But father, hear the good points of my life
In Delphi: leisure first of all, most dear
To any man, the friendly people, no one   635
To thrust me rudely from my path; to yield,
Give elbow room to those beneath us is

Intolerable. Then I was busy with
My prayers to gods or talk with men,
Serving the happy, not the discontented.
I was receiving guests or sending them   640
Away again, a fresh face always smiling
On fresh faces. I had what men should pray,
Even against their will, to have: duty
And inclination both contrived to make
Me righteous to god. When I compare the two,   645
Father, I think I am more happy here.
Let me live here. Delight in splendor is
No more than happiness with little: for both
Have their appeal.

Chorus (aside)
    Well have you spoken if indeed your words
    Mean happiness for her I love.

Xuthus
    No more of this! Learn to enjoy success.   650
    Let us inaugurate our life together
    By holding here, where I have found my son,
    A public banquet, and make the sacrifices
    Omitted at your birth. I will pretend
    To bring you to my house, a guest, and give
    A feast for you; and then take you along   655
    With me to Athens, not as my son but as
    A visitor. I do not want to hurt
    My childless wife with my own happiness.
    But when I think the time is ripe, I will
    Persuade my wife to give consent to your
    Assumption of my rule.   660
        Your name shall be Ion, a name to fit
    Your destiny; you were the first to meet
    Me coming from Apollo's shrine. But now
    Collect your friends together, say farewell
    With feast and sacrifice, before you leave   665

This town of Delphi. And, you women slaves,
I order you, say nothing of our plans.
To tell my wife will mean your death.

Ion

Yes, I will go. But one piece of good luck
Eludes me still: unless I find my mother,
My life is worthless. If I may do so,   670
I pray my mother is Athenian,
So that through her I may have rights of speech.
For when a stranger comes into a city
Of pure blood, though in name a citizen,
His mouth remains a slave: he has no right
Of speech.   675

                                        (*Exeunt.*)

Chorus

STROPHE

I see tears and mourning
Triumphant, a sorrowful entrance,
When the queen hears of the son,
The blessing bestowed on her husband
Alone, still childless herself.   680
O Latona's prophetic son, what reply have you chanted?
From where came this child, reared
In your temple, and who is his mother?
This oracle does not please me.
    There may be a fraud.   685
        I fear the issue
        Of this encounter.
For these are strange matters,   690
A strange command on my silence.
Treachery and chance combine
In this boy of an alien blood.
        Who will deny it?

ANTISTROPHE

My friends, shall we clearly   695
Cry out in the ears of my mistress

Blame upon him who alone
Afforded her hope she could share?
Now she is maimed by his joy.
She is falling to gray age, he does not honor his love.   700
  A stranger he came, wretch,
To the house, and betrays the fortune
Bestowed. He wronged her.—Die then!
    And may he not gain
      From god the prayer   705
    He sends with incense
Ablaze on bright altars.
He shall be sure of my feeling,
How much I love the queen.   710
The new father and son are now near
    To their new banquet.

EPODE

O the ridge of the rocks of Parnassus
Which hold in the skies the watchtower   715
Where Bacchus holds the two-flamed
Torch, leaping lightly with his
Nighttime wandering Bacchanals:
    Let the boy never see my city,
    Let him die and leave his new life.   720
  A city in trouble has reason
  To welcome the coming of strangers.
  But Erechtheus, our ancient founder,
    United us long ago.

*(Creusa enters with an Old Man, a slave and trusted servant
of the family. They begin to climb the temple steps,
Creusa supporting him.)*

Creusa
  Erechtheus, my father, long before he died   725
  Made you the guardian of his children: *(pauses)*
  Come up with me to Phoebus' oracle
  To share my pleasure if his prophecy
  Gives hope of children; since it is a joy

To share success with those we love; and if— 730
I pray that they may not—reverses come,
There is a balm in seeing friendly eyes.
And, though I am your mistress, I love you
As if you were my father, as you did
My own.

Old Man
My daughter, you preserve a noble spirit 735
And equal to your noble ancestors:
You have not shamed your fathers, sons of Earth.
Give me your help, and bring me to the temple.
The shrine is steep, you know. Support my limbs
And heal my weak old age. 740

Creusa
Come then. Be careful how you place your feet.

Old Man (as he stumbles)
You see. My mind is nimbler than my feet.

Creusa
Lean with your staff upon the path around.

Old Man
And that is blind now when my eyes are weak.

Creusa
Yes, true. But fight against your weariness. 745

Old Man
I do. But now I have no strength to summon.

> (He turns slowly and with Creusa's help settles himself on the
> temple steps, looking toward the audience. They
> are now face to face with the Chorus.
> Creusa addresses the Chorus.)

Creusa
You women, faithful servants of my loom
And shuttle, what hope of children did my husband
Receive before he left? We came for that.

Tell me; and if the news is good you will   750
Not find your mistress faithless or ungrateful.

Chorus
An evil fate!

Old Man
Your prelude is not one that suits good luck.

Chorus
Unhappy lot!

Old Man
But what is wrong about the oracle?   755

Chorus
What can we do when death is set before us?

Creusa
What strain is this? Why should you be afraid?

Chorus
Are we to speak or not? What shall we do?

Creusa
O speak! You know of some misfortune coming.

Chorus Leader
You shall be told then, even if I die   760
Twice over —You will never have a child
To hold, or take one to your breast.

              (*Creusa sinks down to the steps beside the slave.*)

Creusa
I wish I were dead.

Old Man
Daughter—

Creusa
        O this blow
Is hard, this pain put upon me,
I cannot endure it, my friends.

Old Man
    Hopeless now, my child.

Creusa
                    Yes, ah! yes.   765
        This blow is fatal, a heart-thrust.
        The sorrow has pierced within.

Old Man
    Mourn no more—

Creusa
                    I have reason enough.

Old Man
    Till we know—

Creusa
                    Is there anything to know?   770

Old Man
    —If you alone have this misfortune, or
    Our master too must share the same.

Chorus Leader
    To him Apollo gave a son, but this
    Good luck is his alone, his wife has nothing.   775

Creusa
        One after the other you have cried out my griefs.
            This is the worst to deplore.

Old Man
    And did the oracle concern a living son,
    Or must some woman yet give birth to him?

Chorus Leader
    Phoebus gave him a son already born,   780
    A full-grown youth; and I myself was witness.

Creusa
        How can it be true? No! an incredible thing.
            It is surely fantastic.

Old Man
    Fantastic! Tell me how the oracle   785
    Is carried out, and who the son can be.

Chorus Leader

He gave your husband for a son the one
He should meet first as he came from the temple.

Creusa

Then it is settled.
Mine is the childless part,
The solitary life in a desolate house.

Old Man

Who then was chosen for Xuthus to meet?
And tell me how and where he saw his child.

Chorus Leader

There was a boy who swept the temple here.
You know him? For he is the son.

Creusa

Would that I might fly
Through the gentle air far away
From Greek earth to the evening stars.
Such is my anguish, my friends.

Old Man

What was the name his father gave to him?
You know it? Or does that remain uncertain?

Chorus Leader

He called him Ion, since he met him first.

Old Man

Who is his mother?

Chorus Leader

That I cannot say.
But Xuthus, to tell you all I know, old man,
Has gone away unknown to her, his wife,
To offer in the consecrated tent
A birthday sacrifice, to pledge the bond
Of friendship in a banquet with his son.

Old Man

My lady, we have been betrayed by your
Own husband—for I share your grief; we are

790

795

800

805

Insulted by design, cast from the house   810
Of Erechtheus: this I say not out of hatred,
But rather since I love you more than him:
The foreigner who married you and came
Into the city and your house, received
Your heritage, and now is proved the father
Of children by another—secretly.   815
How secretly I will explain to you.
Aware that you would have no children,
He scorned to suffer equally with you
In this mischance, and had a secret child
By some slave woman, and sent him away
For someone in Delphi to rear. The boy   820
Was dedicated to Apollo's temple,
And there grew in concealment. While the father,
Now knowing that the boy was grown, pressed you
To travel here because you had no child.
And so Apollo did not lie, but he   825
Who has long reared the child. This is his web
Of deceit: discovered, he would lay the blame
Upon the god; if not, to guard against
The blows of time, his plan was to invest
Him with the city's rule. As time went on,
The new name Ion was invented, suiting   830
This trick of meeting him outside the temple.

Chorus Leader
  I hate all evil men who plot injustice,
  Then trick it out with subterfuge. I would
  Prefer as friend a good man ignorant
  Than one more clever who is evil too.   835

Old Man
  Worst shame of all that he should bring into
  Your house a cipher, motherless, the child
  Of some slave woman. For the shame at least
  Would have been open, if, with your consent,

Because you could not bear a child yourself,   840
He had an heir by one highborn. If this
Had been too much, he should have been content
To marry an Aeolian.
    And so you must now act a woman's part:
Kill them, your husband and his son, by sword,
By poison or some trick before death comes   845
To you from them. Unless you act your life
Is lost; for when two enemies have met
Together in a house, the one must be
Unlucky. Now I will help you kill the son: 850
Visit the place where he prepares the feast,
To pay the debt I owe my masters, thus,
To live or die. A slave bears only this
Disgrace: the name. In every other way   855
An honest slave is equal to the free.

Chorus Leader

    I too, dear mistress, want to share your fate,
To die, or live with honor.

Creusa

                    (After a pause, then coming to the front.)
    O my heart, how be silent?
Yet how can I speak of that secret   860
Love, strip myself of all shame?
Is one barrier left still to prevent me?
Whom have I now as my rival in virtue?
Has not my husband become my betrayer?
I am cheated of home, cheated of children,   865
Hopes are gone which I could not achieve,
The hopes of arranging things well
By hiding the facts,
By hiding the birth which brought sorrow.
No! No! But I swear by the starry abode   870
Of Zeus, by the goddess who reigns on our peaks
And by the sacred shore of the lake

Of Tritonis, I will no longer conceal it:
When I have put away the burden,
My heart will be easier.   875
Tears fall from my eyes, and my spirit is sick,
Evilly plotted against by men and by gods;
I will expose them,
Ungrateful betrayers of women.   880

O you who give the seven-toned lyre
A voice which rings out of the lifeless,
Rustic horn the lovely sound
Of the Muses' hymns,
On you, Latona's son, here   885
In daylight I will lay blame.
You came with hair flashing
Gold, as I gathered
Into my cloak flowers ablaze
With their golden light.   890
Clinging to my pale wrists
As I cried for my mother's help
You led me to bed in a cave,
A god and my lover,
With no shame,   895
Submitting to the Cyprian's will.
In misery I bore you
A son, whom in fear of my mother
I placed in that bed
Where you cruelly forced me.   900
Ah! He is lost now,
Snatched as food for birds,
My son and yours; O lost!
    But you play the lyre,   905
    Chanting your paeans.

O hear me, son of Latona,
Who assign your prophecies
From the golden throne

And the temple at earth's center,   910
I will proclaim my words in your ears:
You are an evil lover;
Though you owed no debt
To my husband, you have
Set a son in his house.   915
But my son, yes and yours, hard-hearted,
Is lost, carried away by birds,
The clothes his mother put on him abandoned.
    Delos hates you and the young
    Laurel which grows by the palm   920
    With its delicate leaves, where Latona
    Bore you, a holy child, fruit of Zeus.

(She breaks down, weeping, on the temple steps.
The Chorus gathers round her.)

Chorus Leader
    O what a store of miseries is now
    Disclosed; who could but weep at hearing them?

Old Man
    O child, your face has riveted my gaze,   925
    My reason is distracted. For just when
    I banished from my heart a wave of trouble,
    A second rose at the stern, caused by the words
    You spoke about your present woes, before
    You trod the evil path of other sorrows.   930
    What do you say? What child is this you claim
    To bear? Where in the city did you put
    This welcome corpse for beasts? Tell me again.

Creusa
    I will tell you, although I feel ashamed.

Old Man
    Yes, I know how to feel with friends in trouble.   935

Creusa
    Then listen. You know the cave which lies above
    The north of Cecrops' hill, its name Long Rocks?

Old Man

I know. Pan's altars and his shrine are near.

Creusa

It was there I endured a fearful trial.

Old Man

Yes? My tears spring to meet your words.   940

Creusa

Phoebus became my lover against my will.

Old Man

My child, could that have been the thing I heard?

Creusa

I shall acknowledge truth if you tell me.

Old Man

When you were suffering from a secret illness?

Creusa

That was the sorrow which I now reveal.   945

Old Man

How did you hide this union with Apollo?

Creusa

I had a child.—Please hear my story out.

Old Man

But where, who helped you? Or were you alone?

Creusa

Alone in that cave where I met Apollo.

Old Man

Where is the child? You need not be childless.   950

Creusa

Dead. He was left for beasts to prey upon.

Old Man

Dead? Then Phoebus was false, gave you no help?

Creusa

He did not help. The child grew up in Hades.

Old Man

But who exposed the child? Of course not you?

Creusa

I did: I wrapped him in my robes at night.   955

Old Man

And there was no accomplice in your deed?

Creusa

No, nothing but the silence and my grief.

Old Man

How could you leave your child there, in the cave?

Creusa

How, but with many tender words of pity?—

Old Man

Ah, you were harsh; Apollo harsher still.   960

Creusa

If you had seen the child stretch out his hands!

Old Man

To find your breast, lie in your arms?

Creusa

To find what I was cruelly refusing.

Old Man

But why did you decide to expose your child?

Creusa

Because I hoped the god would save his own.   965

Old Man

A storm embroils the fortunes of your house.

(A pause.)

Creusa

Why do you hide your head, old man, why weep?

Old Man

I see your father and yourself so stricken.

Creusa

Such is man's life. All things must change.

(*A pause, as the Old Man leads Creusa to the front of the stage.*)

Old Man

My child, let us no longer cling to tears.   970

Creusa

What can I do? For pain has no resource.

Old Man

Avenge yourself on him who wronged you first.

Creusa

How can a mortal fight immortal power?

Old Man

Burn down Apollo's sacred oracle.

Creusa

I am afraid.—I have enough of sorrow.   975

Old Man

Then kill your husband. This is in your power.

Creusa

He was once loyal, and I honor that.

Old Man

The son then who has come to menace you.

Creusa

But how? If only I might! I would do that!

Old Man

By putting swords in your attendants' hands.   980

(*A pause.*)

Creusa

Let us begin. But where can it be done?

Old Man

The sacred tent, where he is feasting friends.

Creusa

Murder is flagrant; slaves are poor support.

Old Man (*despairingly*)
   You play the coward; come, give me your plan now.
                     (*A pause, as she prepares to explain her scheme; she goes
                        near to him, speaking softly and urgently, as if
                        to emphasize her own resolution.*)

Creusa
   Yes, I have something which is sure and subtle.   985

Old Man
   And I can help in both these ways.

Creusa
   Then listen. You know the war fought by Earth's sons?

Old Man
   When giants fought against the gods at Phlegra.

Creusa
   Earth there produced an awful monster, Gorgon.

Old Man
   To harass all the gods and help her children?   990

Creusa
   Yes, but destroyed by Zeus's daughter Pallas.

Old Man
   Is this the tale which I have heard before?

Creusa
   Yes, that she wears its skin upon her breast.   995

Old Man
   Athene's armor which they call her aegis?

Creusa
   So called from how she rushed into the battle.

Old Man
   What was the form of this barbaric thing?

Creusa
   A breastplate armed with serpent coils.
                              (*An impatient pause.*)

Old Man

But my child, what harm can this do to your foes?

Creusa

You know Erichthonius?—Of course you must.

Old Man

The founder of your house, the son of Earth.   1000

Creusa

A newborn child, Athene gave to him—

(*She pauses.*)

Old Man

Yes, what is this you hesitate to say?

Creusa (*slowly*)

Two drops of Gorgon's blood.

Old Man

And these have some effect on men?

Creusa

One is poisonous, the other cures disease.   1005

Old Man

But how did she attach them to the child?

Creusa

A golden chain which he gave to my father.

Old Man

And when he died it came to you?

Creusa

Yes, I always wear it on my wrist.

Old Man

How is the twofold gift compounded then?   1010

Creusa

The drop extracted from the hollow vein—

Old Man

How is it to be used? What power has it?

Creusa
It fosters life and keeps away disease.

Old Man
What action does the other of them have?

Creusa
It kills—a poison from the Gorgon's snakes. 1015

Old Man
You carry them apart or mixed together?

Creusa
Apart. For good and evil do not mingle.

Old Man
O my dear child, you have all that you want!

Creusa
By this the boy shall die, and you shall kill him.

Old Man
But when and how? Tell me, it shall be done. 1020

Creusa
In Athens when he comes into my house.

(A pause, as the slave considers.)

Old Man
No, I distrust this plan as you did mine.

Creusa
Why?—Can we both have seen the same weak point?

Old Man
They will accuse you, innocent or guilty.

Creusa
Since foster mothers must be jealous. 1025

Old Man
But kill him now and so deny the crime.

Creusa
And in that way I taste my joy the sooner.

Old Man

And turn his own deceit upon your husband.

Creusa

You know then what to do? Here, take
This golden bracelet from my hand, Athene's   1030
Old gift; go where my husband holds his feast
In secret; when they end the meal, begin
To pour the gods' libation, then drop this,
Under cover of your robe, into
The young man's cup—in his alone, no more.   1035
Reserve the drink for him who would assume
The mastery of my home. Once this is drained,
He will be dead, stay here and never see
Our glorious Athens.

Old Man

Now go to our host's house, and I will do
The task appointed for me.   1040

(Pause.)

Old foot, come now, take on a youthful strength
For work, although the years deny it you.
March with your masters upon the enemy,
And help to kill and cast him from the house.
Right that the fortunate should honor virtue,   1045
But when we wish to harm our enemies
There is no law which can prevent.

(Exeunt.)

Chorus

STROPHE

Demeter's daughter, guarding the roadway, ruling
What wings through the paths of the night
And the daytime, O guide the potion   1050
Of the death-heavy cup
To whom the queen sends it, brew
Of the blood drops from the Gorgon's severed throat,   1055
To him who lifts his presumptuous hand

Against the house of Erechtheus.
  Let no others ever have
  Sway in the city:
  Only the sons of Erechtheus.   1060

ANTISTROPHE

My mistress is planning a death, and if it should fail,
The occasion of action go past,
Now her sole anchor of hope,
She will sharpen a sword
Or fasten a noose to her neck,   1065
Ending sorrow by sorrows, pass down to the realm of change.
For she would never endure to see
Foreigners ruling the house,   1070
  Not while living her eyes
  Still have their clarity—
  She, born of a noble line.

STROPHE

O the shame to many-hymned Dionysus, if by the springs
Where lovely choruses are danced,   1075
Apollo's bastard son shall behold
Unsleeping, keeping the watch,
The torches burning on the festival night,
When the star-faced heavens join in the dance,   1080
With the moon and the fifty Nereids
Who dance in the depths of the sea,
In perennial river-springs,
Honoring the gold-crowned Maid   1085
And her mother, holy Demeter:
  There, where he hopes
  To rule, usurping
  What others have wrought.

ANTISTROPHE

All you poets who raise your unjust strains   1090
Singing the unsanctioned, unholy loves

Of women, see how much we surpass
In virtue the unrighteous race   1095
Of men. Let a song of different strain
Ring out against men, harshly indicting
Their love. For here is one
Of the offspring of Zeus who shows
His ingratitude, refusing   1100
To bring good luck to the house
With his and Creusa's child:
    But yielding to passion
    For another, has found
    A bastard son.   1105

           (*Enter a Servant of Creusa, greatly agitated.*)

Servant
  Women, can you tell me where I may find
  Erechtheus' noble daughter? I have searched
  The city everywhere without success.

Chorus Leader
  What is it, friend? Why are you hurrying?
  What is the message you have brought?   1110

Servant
  They are behind. The Delphian officers are looking
  For her to stone to death.

Chorus Leader
  What do you mean? Have they discovered then
  The secret plot we made to kill the boy?

Servant
  Correct—and you will not be the last to suffer.   1115

Chorus Leader
  How was this scheme, unknown to them, discovered?

Servant
  The god refused to be defiled, and so
  Found means of combating the victory
  Of justice over the unjust.

Chorus Leader

But how? I beg you tell me that: for if
I have to die, I shall die more content   1120
Because I know my fate.

(*The women press nearer to the Servant.*)

Servant

Creusa's husband came out from the shrine
Of Phoebus, and then took his new-found son
Away to join the feast and sacrifice
He was preparing for the gods. Xuthus
Himself was going to the place where   1125
The sacred Bacchanalian fires leap,
To sprinkle the twin crags of Dionysus
With victim's blood for having seen his son.
"My son," he said, "will you stay here and see
That workmen build a tent inclosed on all
Its sides. And if I should be long away,
While sacrificing to the gods of birth,   1130
Begin the banquet with such friends as come."
    He took the victims then and went away.
Ion had the framework built in ritual form
On upright poles without a wall, and paid
Attention to the sun, so that he might   1135
Avoid its midday and its dying rays
Of flame, and measuring a square, its sides
A hundred feet, so that he could invite
All Delphians to the feast. To shade the tent   1140
He took from store some sacred tapestries,
A wonder to behold. And first he cast
Above the roof a wing of cloth, spoil from
The Amazons, which Heracles, the son
Of Zeus, had dedicated to the god.   1145
And there were figures woven in design:
For Uranus was mustering the stars
In heaven's circle; and Helios drove his horses
Toward his dying flame and trailed the star

Which shines bright in the West. While black-robed Night,   1150
Drawn by a pair, urged on her chariot,
Beside the stars kept pace with her. The Pleiades
And Orion, his sword in hand, moved through
The sky's mid-path; and then, above, the Bear
Who turned his golden tail within the vault.
The round full moon threw up her rays, dividing   1155
The month; the Hyades, the guide most sure
For sailors; then light's herald, Dawn, routing
The stars. The sides he draped with tapestries
Also, but of barbarian design.
There were fine ships which fought with Greeks, and creatures,   1160
Half-man, half-beast, and horsemen chasing deer
Or lion hunts. And at the entrance, Cecrops,
His daughters near him, wreathed himself in coils
Of serpents—this a gift which had been given
By some Athenian. Then in the center   1165
He put the golden mixing bowls. A herald
Then went and announced that any Delphian
Who pleased was free to attend the feast. And when
The tent was full, they wreathed their heads with flowers
And ate the food spread in abundance till
Desire was satisfied. When they had done   1170
With eating, an old man came in and stood
Among the guests, and threw them into laughter
With his officious antics. He poured out water
From jars to wash their hands, or burned
The ooze of myrrh, and put himself in charge   1175
Of golden drinking cups. And when the flutes
Came in together with the bowl which all
Had now to drink, he said, "Enough of these
Small cups, we must have large; the company
Will then be all the sooner in good spirits."   1180
And now they busied themselves with passing gold
And silver cups; but he, as though he meant
To honor his new master, offered him

A chosen cup of wine, and put in this
A fatal poison which they say our mistress   1185
Had given, to have an end of this new son.
And no one knew. But when like all the rest
He held his cup, one of the slaves let fall
Some phrase of evil omen. He had been reared
Among good prophets in the temple, and knew   1190
The sign and ordered them to fill another.
The first libation of the god he emptied
On the ground and told the rest to pour
As he had done. A silence followed when
We filled the sacred bowls with Byblian wine   1195
And water. While this was being done, there came
Into the tent a riotous flight of doves—
They haunt Apollo's shrine and have no fear.
To slake their thirst, they dipped their beaks into
The wine the guests had poured and drew it down   1200
Their well-plumed throats; and all but one were not
Harmed by the god's libation. But she had perched
Where Ion poured his wine and tasted it.
At once her feathered body shook and quivered,
She screamed strange cries of anguish. All the band   1205
Of guests looked on amazed to see her struggles.
She died in her convulsions, her pink claws
And legs relaxed. The son the god foretold
Then stretched his uncloaked arms across the table,
And cried, "Who planned my death? Tell me, old man,   1210
Since you were so officious; you handed me
The drink." He held the old man by the arm
And searched him instantly, so that he might
Convict him in the act. His guilt was proved
And he revealed, compelled against his will,   1215
Creusa's plotting with the poisoned drink.
     The youth bestowed by Loxias collected
The guests, went from the tent without delay,
And took his stand before the Delphian nobles.

"O rulers of the sacred city," he said,   1220
"A foreign woman, daughter of Erechtheus,
 Has tried to poison me." The lords of Delphi
 By many votes decided that my mistress
 Be put to death, thrown from the rock, for planning
 The murder of a sacred person there
 Inside the temple. Now all the city looks   1225
 For her whom misery advanced on this
 Unhappy path. Desire for children caused
 Her visit here to Phoebus, but now her life
 Is lost, and with her life all hopes.

Chorus
 There is no escape, we are doomed,
 No escape from death.   1230
 It has been made clear,
 The libation of Dionysian grapes
 Mingled for murder with blood drops
 From the swift-working viper,
 Clear that in sacrifice to the gods below   1235
 Our lives are set for disaster.
 They will stone my mistress to death.
 What winged flight can I take,
 Down to what dark caverns of the earth
 Can I go to escape the stones of destruction?   1240
 By mounting a chariot
 Drawn by horses with speedy hooves,
 Or the prow of a ship?

 There is no concealment, unless a god wishes
 To withdraw men from sight.   1245
 O unhappy mistress, what sufferings
 Wait for your soul? Shall we not,
 For the will to do harm to our fellows,
 According to justice, suffer ourselves?

                    (*Creusa rushes in, wildly agitated and despairing.*)

Creusa

They are in pursuit, my friends, they want to butcher me; 1250
By the judgment of the Pythian vote my life is forfeit.

Chorus Leader

Yes, we know in what distress you are, unhappy woman.

Creusa

Where can I find refuge then? For I have evaded them
By a trick, just left the house in time to save my life.

Chorus Leader

Where, but at the altar?

Creusa

What advantage will that give me? 1255

Chorus Leader

God defends the suppliant.

Creusa

Yes, but the law condemns me.

Chorus Leader

They must seize you first.

Creusa

And here my bitter rivals come,
Pressing on with sword in hand.

Chorus Leader

Sit at the altar now.
For if you die sitting there, your killers will be made
Guilty of your blood. Now destiny must be endured. 1260

(*Creusa retires quickly to the altar at the back of the stage. She
has hardly had time to sit there before Ion, sword in hand,
comes in at the head of a group of armed men, closely
followed by a crowd of Delphians. For some time
he is not aware that Creusa is at the altar.*)

Ion

O Cephisus, her bull-shaped ancestor,
What viper or what serpent glancing out
A deadly flame of fire did you beget

In her, this woman who will balk at nothing,
Match for the Gorgon drops with which she tried   1265
To poison me! Take hold of her and let
Parnassus' top, when like a quoit she bounds
From rock to rock, comb out those perfect tresses.
    Luck favored me before I went to Athens
To fall a victim to a stepmother.   1270
For here, among my friends I learnt to measure
Your mind, your menace, and your enmity.
But if I had been trapped inside your house,
You would have sent me straight to death.

       (He suddenly catches sight of Creusa cowering
       at the altar. He strides up to her.)

    The altar will not save you, nor Apollo's   1275
House, since my greater pity is reserved
For myself and my mother. For although
She is not here, my thought of her is constant.

       (He appeals to the people with him.)
You see her treachery—how she can twist
One scheme upon another! She has fled
To cower at the god's own altar, hoping   1280
Thus to avoid her penalty for wrong.

Creusa
    I warn you not to kill me—and I speak
    Not only for myself but for the god
    Who guards this place.

Ion
    What can you have in common with the god?

Creusa
    My body is his to save, a sacred charge.   1285

Ion
    You tried to poison me and I was his.

Creusa
    No longer his; for you had found your father.

Ion

I belonged to Phoebus till my father came.

Creusa

But then no more. Now I belong to him.

Ion

Yes, but I had the piety you lack.   1290

Creusa

I tried to kill the enemy of my house.

Ion

I did not march upon your land with arms.

Creusa

You tried to set Erechtheus' house in flames!

Ion

What fiery flame, what torches did I carry?

Creusa

You hoped to force possession of my home.   1295

Ion

My father's gift—the land he gained himself.

Creusa

How can Aeolians share Athenian land?

Ion

Because he saved it, not with words, but arms.

Creusa

An ally need not own the land he helps!

Ion

You planned my death through fear of my intentions?   1300

Creusa

To save my life in case you ceased intending.

Ion

Childless yourself, you envied my father's child.

Creusa

So you will snatch those homes without an heir?

Ion

Had I no right to share my father's state?

Creusa

A shield and spear, these are your sole possessions.   1305

(Ion loses his temper.)

Ion

Come, leave the altar and the shrine of god.

Creusa

(Her moral indignation yielding to spite.)

Go, find your mother and give her advice.

Ion

While your attempted murder goes unpunished?

Creusa

Not if you wish to kill me in the shrine.

(She grasps the wreaths on the altar as if in supplication.)

Ion

What pleasure can the god's wreaths give to death?   1310

Creusa

I shall thus injure one who injured me.

Ion

O this is monstrous! The laws of god for men
Are not well made, their judgment is unwise.
The unjust should not have the right of refuge
At altars, but be driven away. For gods   1315
Are soiled by the touch of wicked hands. The just—
The injured man, should have this sanctuary.
Instead both good and bad alike all come,
Receiving equal treatment from the gods.

(The Pythian Priestess now enters from the temple. She is old
and very dignified, wearing long white robes fastened by
a golden girdle at the waist; on her head is a wreath
of bay leaves and the riband or fillet which is the
sign of her office. She is carrying a cradle
wrapped in bands of wool.)

Priestess

    O stop, my son. For I, the prophetess   1320
    Of Phoebus, chosen by all the Delphians
    To keep the tripod's ancient law, have left
    The seat of prophecy to pass these bounds.

                      (*Ion greets her with great respect.*)

Ion

    Dear mother, hail! Mother in all but name.

Priestess

    Then let me be so called. It pleases me.   1325

Ion

    You heard how she had planned to murder me?

Priestess

    I heard—but your own cruelty is sinful.

Ion

    Have I no right to kill a murderer?

Priestess

    Wives are unkind to children not their own.

Ion

    As we can be ill used by them.   1330

Priestess

    No. When you leave the temple for your country—

Ion

    What must I do? What is your advice?

Priestess

    Go into Athens, with good omens.

Ion

    All men are pure who kill their enemies.

Priestess

    No more of that.—Hear what I have to say.   1335

Ion

    Then speak. Your message could not be unfriendly.

Priestess

You see the basket I am carrying?

Ion

I see an ancient cradle bound with wool.

Priestess

I picked you up in this, a newborn child.

Ion

What do you say? This tale is new to me.   1340

Priestess

I kept it secret. Now I can reveal it.

Ion

How have you kept it from me all these years?

Priestess

The god desired to hold you as his servant.

Ion

And now he does not wish it? How can I know?

Priestess

Revealing your father, he bids you go from here.   1345

Ion

Why did you keep the cradle? Was that an order?

Priestess

Apollo put the thought into my mind.—

Ion

What thought? Tell me. I want to hear the end.

Priestess

To keep what I had found until this time.

Ion

And does it bring me any help?—or harm?   1350

Priestess

The swaddling clothes you wore are kept inside.

Ion

These clues you bring will help to find my mother.

Priestess
   Which now the god desires—though not before.

Ion
   This is indeed a day of happy signs!

(She offers him the cradle.)

Priestess
   Take this with you—and now look for your mother.   1355

Ion

(Taking the cradle.)
   Throughout all Asia, to Europe's boundaries!

Priestess
   That is your own affair. I reared you, child,
   For Phoebus' sake, and these restore to you,
   Which he wished me to take and keep, although
   Without express command. Why he so wished   1360
   I cannot say. There was no man who knew
   That I had these or where they were concealed.
   And now farewell. I kiss you as my son.

(She embraces him. She turns and takes a few steps toward the
   temple entrance. Then she faces him again, to prolong
   her farewell with a few last words of advice.)

   As for the search, begin it as you ought:
   Your mother might have been a Delphian girl   1365
   Who left you at the temple; inquire here first,
   And then elsewhere in Greece. Now you have heard
   All that we have to say—Apollo, who had
   An interest in your fate, and I myself.

(She leaves the stage through the temple door.)

Ion

(Putting his hands to his face.)
   O how the tears well from my eyes whenever
   My mind goes back to the time when the woman   1370
   Who gave me birth, the child of secret love,
   Disposed of me by stealth, and kept me from

Her breast. Instead, unnamed, I had a life
Of service in Apollo's house; and fate
Was cruel, though the god was kind. I was
Deprived of my dear mother's love throughout
The time I might have lain content and happy,   1375
Held in her arms. My mother suffered too;
She lost the joy a child can bring.

                                    And now
I will resign the cradle as a gift   1380
To god to ward away unpleasant news.
If by some chance my mother were a slave,
To find her would be worse than ignorance.
O Phoebus, to your shrine I dedicate—
    And yet, what does this mean? It is against   1385
The god's own wish; he has preserved for me
My mother's tokens. I must have the courage
To open it. I cannot shun my fate.
O sacred bands and ties which guard my precious
Tokens, what secret do you hide from me?   1390

                    (*He unties the bands of wool from the cradle.*)
A miracle! See how the cradle's covering
Is still unworn; the wicker is not decayed,
Yet years have passed since they were put away.

                    (*Creusa is trembling with excitement, her eyes
                    riveted upon the cradle.*)
Creusa
But what is this I see—beyond my hopes?   1395

Ion
Silence. You were my enemy before.

                    (*Creusa controls her excitement with a great effort and gradually
                    raises herself to a standing position by the altar. The
                    crowd of Delphians, her own women, and Ion
                    all gaze toward her in tense silence.*)

Creusa
This is no time for silence. Do not try
To check me. In that cradle I exposed

You then, my son, a newborn child,
Where the Long Rocks hang over Cecrops' cave.   1400
I will desert the altar even though
I have to die.

> (*She rushes away from the altar, runs up to Ion,*
> *and throws her arms round his neck.*)

Ion
Seize her! God's madness has made her leap away
From the altar's images. Now bind her arms.

Creusa
Go on and kill me. I will not lose you,
The cradle, or the tokens it contains.   1405

Ion
O hypocrite to cheat me with a trick!

Creusa
Oh no! You have found one who loves you.

Ion
What, you love me?—And try a secret murder?

Creusa
You are my son: a mother must love her son.

Ion
Stop spinning lies.—For I am sure to have you.   1410

> (*Decides to trick her.*)

Creusa
O do so then! That is my aim, my son.

Ion
This cradle—has it anything inside?

Creusa
It has the things you wore when I exposed you.

Ion
And can you give their names before you see them?

Creusa
I can; and, if I fail, consent to die.   1415

Ion

   Then speak. Your audacity is strange indeed.
          (He opens the cradle, standing far enough away from Creusa
                                    to prevent her seeing inside it.)

Creusa

   Look for the weaving which I did in childhood.

Ion

   Describe it; girls do many kinds of work.

Creusa

   It is unfinished, a kind of trial piece.

Ion

   And its design—You cannot cheat me there.   1420

Creusa

   There is a Gorgon in the center part.

Ion (aside)

   O Zeus! What fate is this to track us down!

Creusa

   The stuff is fringed with serpents like an aegis.

Ion

   And here it is—found like an oracle!

Creusa

   The loomwork of a girl—so long ago.   1425

Ion

   And anything else? Or will your luck fail now?

Creusa

   Serpents, the custom of our golden race.

Ion

   Athene's gift, who bids you wear them?

Creusa

   Yes, in memory of Erichthonius.

Ion

   What do they do with this gold ornament?   1430

Creusa
It is a necklace for a newborn child.

Ion
Yes, here they are.

(*Shows them. He is now anxious for her success.*)
I long to know the third.

Creusa
I put an olive wreath around you, from
The tree Athene first planted on the rock;
If that is there, it has not lost its green,   1435
But flourishes because the tree is holy.

(*Ion, quite convinced, throws himself into his mother's arms.*)

Ion
O dearest mother, what happiness to see you,
To kiss you, and know that you are happy!

Creusa
O child! O light more welcome than the Sun.
—The god forgives me—I have you in my arms.   1440
I have found you against all my hopes,
Whom I thought underground in the world
Of Persephone's shades.

Ion
Dear mother, yes, you have me in your arms,
Who died and now have come to you alive.

Creusa
O radiant heaven's expanse,   1445
How can I speak or cry
My joy? How have I met
Unimagined delight, and why
Am I made happy?

Ion
There was no more unlikely chance than this,   1450
To find that I am, after all, your son.

Creusa

    I am trembling with fear.

Ion

    That I am lost, although you hold me now?

Creusa

    Yes, since I had cast all hope away.
    But tell me, priestess, from where
    Did you take the child to your arms?
    Whose hand brought him to Apollo's house?   1455

Ion

    It was the work of god. But as we have suffered
    Before, so now we must enjoy our fortune.

Creusa

    My child, you were born in tears,
    In sorrow torn from your mother.
    But now I can breathe on your cheek,   1460
    And am blessed with tender joy.

Ion

    I have no need to speak. You speak for both.

Creusa

    I am childless no longer,
    No longer without an heir.
    The hearth is restored to the home,
    The rulers return to the land,
    And Erechtheus is young once more;   1465
    Now the house is delivered from night
    And looks up to the rays of the sun.

Ion

    Mother, my father should be here with me
    To share the happiness I bring you both.

Creusa

    My child, my child—   1470
    How am I put to shame!

Ion
> Yes?—Tell me.—

Creusa
> You do not know your father.

Ion
> So I was born before your marriage then?

Creusa
> The marriage which gave you birth
> Saw no torches or dancing, my son. 1475

Ion
> A bastard son—My father? Tell me that.

Creusa
> Athene who slew the Gorgon,
> I call her to witness—

Ion
> Why this beginning?

Creusa
> By the rocks where the nightingales sing, 1480
> Apollo—

Ion
> Why name Apollo?

Creusa
> Became my lover in secret—

Ion
> Speak on; for what you say will make me happy. 1485

Creusa
> When the time passed, I bore you,
> The unknown child of Apollo.

Ion
> How welcome this news is—if it is true.

Creusa
> And these were your swaddling clothes;
> In fear of my mother I wrapped you 1490

In them, the careless work of a girl
At her loom.
I gave you no milk,
You were not washed with my hands,
But in a deserted cave,
A prey for the beaks of birds,   1495
Delivered to death.

Ion

O mother, what horror you dared.

Creusa

Myself in the bondage of fear,
I was casting away your life,
But against my will.

Ion

And I attempted an impious murder.   1500

Creusa

Fate drove us hard in the past,
Just now oppressed us again.
There is no harbor of peace
From the changing waves of joy and despair.   1505
The wind's course veers.
Let it rest. We have endured
Sorrows enough. O my son,
Pray for a favoring breeze
Of rescue from trouble.

Chorus Leader

From what we have seen happen here, no man   1510
Should ever think that any chance is hopeless.

(A pause. Ion is afflicted with doubt.)

Ion

O Fortune, who has already changed the lives
Of countless men from misery to joy,
How near I was to killing my own mother,
How near myself to undeserved disaster.   1515

(Pause.)

But do the sun's bright rays in daily course
Illumine such events as this—all this?

(Pause, as he turns to his mother.)

It was so good at last to find you, mother,
And I can cast no blame upon my birth.
But there is something else I wish to say   1520
To you alone. Come here with me; my words
Are for your ear; your answer shall be hidden.

(He draws her aside.)

Now tell me, mother—are you not, deceived
As young girls are in love affairs kept secret,
Now laying blame upon the god, and say,   1525
Attempting to escape the shame I brought,
That Phoebus is my father, though in fact
He is no god at all?

Creusa

No, by Athene, Goddess of Victory,
Who in her chariot fought by Zeus's side
Against the Giant race, my son, your father
Was not a mortal, but the very god   1530
Who reared you, Loxias.

Ion

If this is true, why give his son to others,
Why does he say that Xuthus is my father?

Creusa

No, he does not; you are his son, a gift
Bestowed by him on Xuthus, just as a man   1535
Might give a friend his son to be his heir.

Ion

But, mother, does Apollo tell the truth,
Or is the oracle false? With some good reason
That question troubles me.

Creusa

   Then listen. This is what I think, my son:
   It is for your own good that Loxias   1540
   Is placing you within a noble house.
   Acknowledged as his son, you would have lost
   All hope of heritage or father's name.
   What chance had you when I concealed
   The truth, and even planned your death in secret?
   And so to help you he is giving you
   Another father.   1545

Ion

   My question cannot be so lightly answered;
   No, I will ask Apollo in his temple
   If I am his, or born of man.

               (As he steps toward the temple, he sees the goddess)
                             Athene appearing above it.)

   Ah!
   What goddess shows her face above the temple
   To look toward the sun? O mother, let us fly.   1550
   We should not see the gods unless the right
   Is given to us.

                 (All on the stage bow their heads to the ground
                    and step backward from the temple.)

Athene

   No, stay. I am no enemy to flee,
   But well-disposed in Delphi as in Athens.
   I am Athene, whose name your city bears: 1555
   I have come here in haste, sent by Apollo,
   Who did not think it right to come himself
   Before you, lest he should be blamed for what
   Has happened in the past; he has sent me
   To give his message:
              This woman is your mother,   1560
   Your father is Apollo; the one you know
   Received you as a gift, and not because

You are his son; and this was done with purpose,
To find you an established place among
A noble house. But when this plan he made
Was open and laid bare, he was afraid
Your mother's scheme of murder would succeed,
Or she be killed by you, and found some means   1565
Of rescue; but for this he would have kept
The secret longer and in Athens revealed
Creusa as the mother and himself
The father of his child. But I must end
My task and tell the purpose of my journey.
Now hear Apollo's revelations.   1570
                   Creusa,
Go with your son to Cecrops' land, and then
Appoint him to the royal throne; for since
He is descended from Erechtheus, he has
The right to rule my land: and he shall be
Renowned through Greece. His sons, four branches from   1575
One stock, shall name the country and its peoples,
Divided in their tribes, who live about my rock.
The first shall be named Geleon, the tribe
Of Hopletes second, then Argades, and one   1580
Aegicores, the name from my own aegis.
At the appointed time, the children born
Of them shall colonize the Cyclades,
Possess the island cities and the coasts,
And thus give strength to my own land of Athens.
They shall live in the two broad plains of Asia
And Europe, which lie on either side the straits,   1585
Becoming famous under this boy's name,
Ionians. Moreover, you and Xuthus
Are promised children. First Dorus, whose name
Shall cause the Dorians to be hymned throughout   1590
The land of Pelops. Then Achaeus, king
Of that sea coast near Rhion, who shall mark
A people with his name.

Apollo then
Has managed all things well. He made your labor   1595
Easy, so that your parents should not know;
And when the child was born and you exposed
Him in his swaddling clothes, he ordered Hermes
To take him in his arms and bring him here,
And would not let him die, but reared him.   1600
But tell no one that Ion is your son,
And Xuthus will be happy in his belief,
While you may go away, Creusa, sure
Of your own blessings.—Now farewell;
You are delivered of your present evil,
The future holds good fortune.   1605

Ion (ironically)
    O Athene, child of mighty Zeus, we have received
    What you say on trust. And I believe myself Apollo's
    And Creusa's son—though that was credible before.

               (To the end of the scene Ion stands in silence.)

Creusa
    Listen to my tribute. Though before I gave no praise,
    Now I praise Apollo. For the son he had neglected   1610
    Is restored to me; and now this oracle, these doors,
    Wear a friendly look, though they were hateful in the past.
    Joyfully I cling to them and bid farewell.

Athene
    I approve this change, this praise of him. The gods perhaps
    Move to action late, but in the end they show their strength. 1615

Creusa
    Son, now let us go.

Athene
              Yes, go, and I will follow you.

Creusa
    Welcome guardian of our journey, one who loves the city.

Athene (to Ion)
    Mount the ancient throne.

        (Ion is silent. There is an embarrassing pause.)

Creusa
        That is a worthy prize for me.

    (The actors slowly move off the stage in procession.
        Athene disappears.)

Chorus
        (To the temple.)
    O Apollo, son of Zeus and Leto, now farewell.

        (To the audience.)
He whose house is pressed by trouble should respect the gods,   1620
So preserving courage. For at last good men are honored,
Evil men by their own nature cannot ever prosper.

        (Exeunt.)